CONSIDER THE ISSUES

Second Edition
Advanced Listening and
Critical Thinking Skills

Carol Numrich

in cooperation with National Public Radio

Longman

Consider the Issues: Advanced Listening and Critical Thinking Skills, Second Edition

Longman, 10 Bank Street, White Plains, NY 10606

Photo Credits appear on page 164.

Editorial Director: Joanne Dresner
Acquisitions Editor: Allen Ascher
Development Editor: Françoise Leffler
Production: Karen Philippidis, Nik Winter
Text Design: Curt Belshe
Cover Design: Curt Belshe

Library of Congress Cataloging in Publication Data

Numrich, Carol.
    Consider the issues : advanced listening and critical thinking skills / Carol Numrich, in
cooperation with National Public Radio.
    -2nd ed.
        p.   cm.
    ISBN 0-201-82529-5 (pbk.)
        1. English language—Textbooks for foreign speakers.   2. Current events—Problems,
exercises, etc.   3. Critical thinking.   4. Listening.   I. National Public Radio (U.S.)
II. Title.
PE1128.N8   1995   94-33391
428.3´4—dc20   CIP

3 4 5 6 7 8 9 10-CRS-0099989796

CONTENTS

INTRODUCTION

Consider the Issues: *Advanced Listening and Critical Thinking Skills* consists of twelve authentic radio interviews and reports from National Public Radio. The broadcasts were taken from "All Things Considered," "Weekend All Things Considered," "Living on Earth," and "Morning Edition."

Designed for high-intermediate or advanced students of English as a second language, the text presents an integrated approach to developing listening comprehension and critical thinking skills. By using material produced for the native speaker, the listening selections provide content that is interesting, relevant, and educational. At the same time, it exposes the nonnative speaker to unedited language, including the hesitations, redundancies, and various dialectal patterns that occur in everyday speech.

Each unit presents either a dialogue or a discussion of an issue of international appeal. The students gain an understanding of American values and culture as they develop their listening skills. Throughout each unit, students are encouraged to use the language and concepts presented in the listening material and to reevaluate their point of view.

The second edition of **Consider the Issues** offers six new units based on broadcasts about compelling contemporary topics. In addition, a new note-taking feature helps students consolidate the ideas from the broadcast in order to apply them in follow-up activities.

SUGGESTIONS FOR USE

The exercises are designed to stimulate an interest in the material by drawing on students' previous knowledge and opinions and by aiding comprehension through vocabulary and guided listening exercises. In a variety of discussion activities, the students finally integrate new information with previously held opinions.

1 Predicting

In this exercise, students are asked to read the title of the interview or report and predict the content of the unit. This exercise should take a very short time, two or three minutes.

Some of the titles require an understanding of vocabulary or idiomatic expressions that the teacher may want to explain to the students. The ideas generated by the students could be written on the chalkboard. Once the students have listened to the interview or report, they can then verify their predictions.

2   Think Ahead

Before listening to the tape, students are asked to discuss the issues to be presented in the interview or report. In groups of four or five, the students discuss their answers to general questions or react to statements that include ideas from the broadcast. The students draw on their own knowledge or experience for this activity. It is likely that students will have different opinions, and the discussion, especially with a verbal class, could become quite lengthy. It is recommended that the teacher limit this discussion to ten or fifteen minutes, so as not to exhaust the subject prior to the listening activities.

3   Vocabulary

In this section, three types of exercises are presented to prepare the students for vocabulary and expressions used in the listening selection.

Vocabulary in a reading text. In these exercises, vocabulary is presented in a reading passage that also introduces some of the ideas from the broadcast. The students should read through the text once for global comprehension. Then, as they reread the text, they match the vocabulary items with synonyms or short definitions. The meaning of the new words may be derived from context clues, from general knowledge of the language, or from the dictionary.

Vocabulary in sentences. In these exercises, vocabulary is presented in sentences that relate to the ideas in the listening selection. Context clues are provided in each sentence. The students should first try to guess the meaning of these words by supplying their own definition or another word that they think has similar meaning. Although the students may not be sure of the exact meaning, they should be encouraged to guess. This will lead them to a better understanding of the new words. Once they have tried to determine the meaning of these words through context, they match the words with definitions or synonyms.

Vocabulary in word groups. These exercises focus on the relationship between specific vocabulary items from the listening selection and other words. A set of three words follows a given vocabulary item; in each set, two words have a similar meaning to the vocabulary item. It is suggested that students work together to discuss what they know about these words. Through these discussions, they will begin to recognize roots and prefixes and how these words relate to each other. The students should be encouraged to use their dictionaries for this exercise.

4   Task Listening

This exercise presents the students with a global comprehension task before asking them to focus on more specific information in the listening selection. The "task" is purposely simple to help students focus on an important point in the recorded material. Consequently, most of the students should be able to answer the questions after the first listening.

5   Listening for Main Ideas

The second time students hear the recorded material, they are given questions or key words to guide them in comprehending the main ideas of the listening selection. Each interview or report has between three and five main ideas used to divide the selection into parts. Each part is introduced by a beep on the tape. The students are asked to write complete statements of the main ideas. The teacher should stop the tape at the sound of the beep to allow the students time to write. The students may then compare their statements to see whether they have understood the relevant information. Only one listening is usually required for this exercise; however, some classes may need to listen twice in order to capture all the information. The teacher may want to ask individual students to write the ideas on the chalkboard. From these statements, the class can discuss the ones that represent the best expression of the main points.

6   Listening for Details

In the third listening, the students are asked to focus on detailed information. They are first asked to read either true-and-false statements or multiple-choice questions. The teacher should clarify any items that the students do not understand. Then each part of the recording is played. The students choose the correct answers as they listen, thus evaluating their comprehension. Finally, in pairs, they compare answers. The teacher should encourage the students to defend their answers based on their comprehension. They should also be encouraged to use the language from the tape to convince the other students of the accuracy of their answers. There will certainly be disagreements over some of the answers; the discussions will help focus attention on the information needed to answer the questions correctly. By listening to each part another time, the students generally recognize this information. Once again, they should be asked to agree on their answers. If there are still misunderstandings, the tape should be played a third time, with the teacher verifying the answers and pointing out where the information is heard on the tape.

7 Looking at Language

In this exercise, an interesting point of language from the recorded material is presented in isolation, as a further aid to comprehension. The students are asked to listen to a segment from the listening selection and to focus on this use of language in context. Then, through discussions and exercises, the students practice the language in a different context. These exercises are not meant to be exhaustive but rather to point out an interesting use of language. The teacher may want to supplement this exercise.

8 Follow-up Activities

In this section, three activities are presented. The teacher may want to choose only one, or perhaps choose one oral and one writing activity. The students should be encouraged to incorporate in their writing and discussions the vocabulary and concepts that were presented in the interview or report. It is expected that the students will synthesize the information gathered from the broadcast with their own opinions.

Discussion questions. In groups, the students discuss their answers to one or more of the questions. Students will most likely have different points of view, and it is during this discussion that they are given the opportunity to present their views to each other.

Composition questions. These questions give the students the opportunity to react in writing to the interview or report.

Interactive processing activities. Each activity begins with an optional listening and note-taking exercise in which the students listen again to the interview or report for important details. By listening with a particular focus, they will be better prepared to complete the final activities. These final activities consist of debates, case studies, roleplays, values clarification exercises, and other activities in which the students must solve problems or develop ideas that recycle the language and concepts in the interviews and reports. During these activities, the students will have an opportunity to creatively examine their beliefs about the issues presented.

ACKNOWLEDGMENTS

The second edition of *Consider the Issues* is dedicated to the memory of Jim Lydon, whose vision and support were instrumental in creating the original text.

The development and realization of this project would never have been possible without the help, support, and shared ideas of many people. I wish to give special thanks to the following friends and colleagues for providing important insights into the content of this material:

Eric Cooper, Richard Duffy, John Een, Tess Ferree, Robert Hertzig, Sherwin Kizner, Bo Knepp, Sherry Preiss, Stratten Ray, Joel Rosenfeld, Paul Rudder, and Janice Sartori.

I am particularly indebted to Sherry Preiss and Kim Sanabria for piloting new material for the second edition of this book. Their feedback was extremely helpful in the development of these new units. I would also like to thank Elaine Cohen, Judy Gilbert, and Ted Scheffler for their comments in editing new units.

In addition, several people were involved in the planning and development of the project. I am indebted to:

Bernice Cohn, Luigi DeMaio, Gloria Gallingane, Stephan Hittman, Suma Kurien, Lou Levi, Robert Oprandy, Peter Thomas, and Linda Tobash.

I am especially grateful to the staff at National Public Radio for their support and encouragement throughout the process of writing this book. I would like to give particular thanks to:

Wendy Blair, Carolyn Gershfeld, Beth Howard, Frederica Kushner, Carol Iannone, Robert Malesky, Christine Malesky, Margot McGann, Elisabeth Sullivan, and Carol Whitehorn.

Finally, without the guidance and support of my editors, this project would never have been realized. I would like to express my gratitude to Joanne Dresner, Allen Ascher, Penny Laporte, Karen Philippidis, and Thomas Finnegan.

GIVE ME MY PLACE TO SMOKE!

1   PREDICTING

From the title, discuss what you think the interview is about.

2   THINK AHEAD

In groups, discuss your answers to the following questions:

1. Is smoking common in your country? Describe a typical smoker there.

2. Is the number of women smokers increasing in your country? Why or why not?

3. Is smoking permitted in most public places in your country? Where is smoking restricted?

3   VOCABULARY

The following words will help you understand the interview. Try to guess the meaning of these words from your knowledge of English, or use your dictionary. In each set of words, cross out the word that does not have a similar meaning. Then compare your answers with those of another student. Discuss the relationship between the words in each set. The first one has been done for you.

1. **secondhand**	used	~~double~~	old
2. **apolitical**	politically involved	politically detached	politically disinterested
3. **cocktail**	mixed drink	alcoholic beverage	after-dinner drink
4. **blabbing**	gossiping	talking foolishly	lecturing
5. **furtively**	openly	secretively	covertly
6. **cognizant**	conscious	intelligent	aware
7. **take a drag**	puff at	pull	inhale
8. **defiance**	relief	resistance	refusal
9. **inflict**	force	impose	soften
10. **patrol**	guard	patron	police
11. **knuckle under**	fight	yield	submit

4	**TASK LISTENING**

Listen to the interview. Find the answer to the following question:

> Who is more tolerant of nonsmokers' attitudes, Peggy or Michael?

5	**LISTENING FOR MAIN IDEAS**

Listen to the interview again. The interview has been divided into five parts, each expressing a main idea. You will hear a beep at the end of each part. Answer the question for each part in a complete sentence. You should have five statements that make a summary of the report. Compare your summary with that of another student.

PART 1   What has changed over the years?

_____

PART 2   How has the behavior of smokers changed in people's homes?

_____

PART 3   How have the smoking habits of smokers changed?

_____

PART 4   In what situations do the smokers feel defiant?

_____

PART 5   How do Michael and Peggy react differently toward people's feelings about smoking?

_____

6   LISTENING FOR DETAILS

*Read the statements for Part 1. Then listen to Part 1 again and decide whether the statements are true or false. As you listen, write **T** or **F** next to each statement. Compare your answers with those of another student. If you disagree, listen again to Part 1.*

PART 1

_____   1. Peggy has smoked for over thirty-five years.

_____   2. Peggy and Michael feel comfortable smoking in their neighborhood bar in Washington, D.C.

_____   3. The EPA[1] report on secondhand smoke[2] will restrict smoking in public places.

_____   4. Peggy used to give more thought to her smoking thirty-five years ago.

_____   5. Peggy thinks the nonsmoking movement is political.

_____   6. Peggy thinks today's attitude toward smoking is similar to other attitudes toward freedom.

Repeat the same procedure for Parts 2–5.

PART 2

_____   7. Fifteen years ago, people offered you an ashtray when you went to their house.

_____   8. Today, Michael finds it awkward to ask for an ashtray.

---

[1] *Environmental Protection Agency:* This means that the report was government funded.
[2] *secondhand smoke*: smoke, exhaled by a smoker, that is inhaled by another person

_____ 9. People used to drink, smoke, and talk at the same time at parties.

_____ 10. Smokers at parties now have to stand at the window or outside the house to smoke.

PART 3

_____ 11. Peggy never lights up a cigarette in someone's office or home.

_____ 12. Michael now blows his smoke straight into the group of people he's with.

_____ 13. Michael looks like a factory when he smokes.

PART 4

_____ 14. Michael has sometimes felt a desire to inflict his habit on others.

_____ 15. Michael feels defiant when someone doesn't want him to smoke in a smoking area.

_____ 16. Michael understood that the man behind him was really uncomfortable with his smoking.

_____ 17. Peggy feels defiant toward anyone who wants to judge her behavior.

PART 5

_____ 18. Michael can understand people who don't want to be around smoke.

_____ 19. Michael lives according to the antismoking rules.

_____ 20. Peggy would only consider going to restaurants that don't allow smoking.

_____ 21. Peggy feels smokers should be given equity.

7 | LOOKING AT LANGUAGE

■ PRESENT PERFECT, PRESENT PERFECT CONTINUOUS, AND SIMPLE PAST

Listen to the following statements from the interview. They describe events that started in the past and continued into the present.

Present perfect continuous:

> My name is Michael, and ***I've been smoking*** for fifteen years.

> My name's Peggy, and ***I've been smoking*** for probably thirty to thirty-five years.

Present perfect:

> ***I've developed*** a whole body language about smoking in groups and in places where it is permissible to smoke.

> ***I've*** never ***felt*** a desire to inflict my habit on someone else.

The verb forms used in these sentences are the present perfect continuous and present perfect. Unlike the past tense, which describes a completed action at a specific time in the past, these tenses are used to describe a state, activity, or repeated action that began in the past and continues into the present time.

Sometimes, however, a present perfect action is finished. By using the present perfect tense, the result of the action is emphasized.

Although the two tenses can often be used interchangeably, the present perfect continuous is often used when the continuation of an action is stressed. It often shows that an activity or state is unfinished.

Notice the form of the present perfect continuous and the present perfect:

Present perfect continuous: Present perfect:

have + ***been*** + (verb) ***-ing***   ***have*** + past participle

Exercise

*Read the following sentences. Use the context of each sentence to determine whether the **simple past**, **present perfect**, or **present perfect continuous** best completes the sentence. Circle the correct verb form.*

1. In recent years, more and more public places _____ smoking.

   a. restricted   b. have been restricting

2. Thirty-five years ago, Peggy _____ a lot of thought to her smoking.

   a. didn't give   b. hasn't given

3. Fifteen years ago, people _____ you an ashtray when you walked into their house.

   a. offered   b. have been offering

4. When Peggy was asked not to smoke in someone's home, she _____ it awkward.

   a. found   b. has found

5. Smoking has become less and less popular. Many of the people Michael sees at parties these days _____ smoking.

   a. gave up   b. have given up

6. During the interview, Michael _____ the smoking style he uses to respect the rights of people who don't want smoke around them.

   a. demonstrated   b. has been demonstrating

7. During the interview, Peggy _____ people to give her her place to smoke.

   a. asked   b. has been asking

8. Peggy and Michael feel that their acceptance as smokers _____.

   a. has been changing   b. has changed

8 | **FOLLOW-UP ACTIVITIES**

■ DISCUSSION QUESTIONS

In groups, discuss your answers to the following questions:

1. Should cigarette smoking be permitted in public places? If so, in which places?

2. Do you think smoking will eventually be made illegal? Are the smoking restrictions in the United States a sign of what will happen in other countries, or are Americans unique in their current reaction to smoking?

3. Do you think tobacco should be classified as a drug?

■ COMPOSITION TOPICS

Choose one of the following topics:

1. Should smokers have the right to smoke in public, and if so, should there be any limits? Write an essay in which you express your opinion.

2. Peggy suggests that there are more "freedoms" that are being limited today in addition to smoking. Do you agree with her? Write an essay in which you discuss those freedoms that are being limited in today's society.

■ DEBATE: SMOKING IN PUBLIC PLACES

A. Taking Notes to Prepare

*Listen to the interview again. Take notes on how attitudes toward smoking have changed over the years. Key phrases and some examples have been provided for you. Use your notes in the **debate** that follows to help you discuss the pros and cons of smoking in public places.*

	Years ago	**Today**
Smokers' attitudes toward their smoking:	• didn't give a lot of thought to it	• keenly aware of others' perceptions • realize it's much less popular
Smoking at people's homes:		
Smoking at parties:		
Smokers' habits:		

B. Debate

For this debate, the class is divided into two teams. The debate will focus on smoking in public places.

Team A will argue in favor of smoking in public places.

> You believe that smokers have the right to smoke in public places. You will argue in favor of providing smoking sections in restaurants, theaters, on public transportation, etc., so that smokers can have the opportunity to smoke if they wish.

Team B will argue in favor of prohibiting smoking in public places.

> You believe that smokers should not have the right to smoke in public places. You will argue in favor of prohibiting smoking in theaters, on public transportation, etc., because you feel it is unpleasant and unhealthy* for nonsmokers even when people smoke in designated areas.

Prepare your arguments. A moderator will lead the debate.

DEBATE PROCEDURES

Team A begins with a three-minute presentation.
Team B then gives a three-minute presentation.
Team A responds to Team B's presentation for three minutes.
Team B responds to Team A's presentation for three minutes.

After the debate, the moderator evaluates the strength of both arguments.

* Reports have shown that secondhand smoke is unhealthy for nonsmokers.
"Give Me My Place to Smoke!" was first broadcast on "All Things Considered," January 9, 1993. The interviewer is Katie Davis.

A WINE THAT'S RAISED SOME STINK

1 PREDICTING

From the title, discuss what you think the interview is about.

2   # THINK AHEAD

In groups, discuss your answers to the following questions:

1. Have you ever tasted a combination of foods or drinks that you thought sounded terrible but was actually quite good?

2. What food or drink does your home town or country produce?

3. How are the products from your town or country marketed for sale in other towns and countries?

3   # VOCABULARY

The following words will help you understand the interview. Try to guess the meaning of these words from your knowledge of English, or use your dictionary. In each set of words, cross out the word that does not have a similar meaning. Then compare your answers with those of another student. Discuss the relationship between the words in each set. The first one has been done for you.

1. **label**	sign	~~top~~	classification
2. **breathless**	short of breath	bad breath	out of breath
3. **derived from**	reproduced	originated	comes from
4. **essence**	perfume	extraction	imitation
5. **fermentation**	chemical change	acidity	transportation
6. **tang**	smell	taste	flavor
7. **pungent**	bitter	sour	sweet
8. **prejudice**	bias	opinion	fact
9. **cuisine**	kitchen	dish	cooking
10. **stuffy**	dull	exciting	formal
11. **colleague**	friend	co-worker	employer

4	**TASK LISTENING**

Listen to the interview. Find the answer to the following question:

> What is this new wine made from?

5	**LISTENING FOR MAIN IDEAS**

Listen to the interview again. The interview has been divided into three parts, each expressing a main idea. You will hear a beep at the end of each part. Answer the question for each part in a complete sentence. You should have three statements that make a summary of the interview. Compare your summary with that of another student.

PART 1   Why did the winery make a wine from garlic?

_____

PART 2   How is garlic wine made?

_____

PART 3   How do people generally react to tasting garlic wine?

_____

6	**LISTENING FOR DETAILS**

Read the questions for Part 1. Then listen to Part 1 again. As you listen, circle the best answer. Compare your answers with those of another student. If you disagree, listen to Part 1 again.

PART 1

1. Where is the new wine considered to be "a first"?

   a. in California

   b. in the United States

   c. in the world

(continued on next page)

2. How do the two wine tasters react to the wine?

   a. It tastes like wine.

   b. It tastes like garlic.

   c. It tastes unusual.

3. What is special about Gilroy, California?

   a. People are serious there.

   b. It's the capital of California.

   c. They grow a lot of garlic there.

4. Which of the following is *not* true about garlic wine?

   a. Its label says it won't give you bad breath.

   b. Many people are ordering it.

   c. It costs five dollars a bottle.

Repeat the same procedure for Parts 2 and 3.

PART 2

5. Why did the Rappazinis decide to make garlic wine?

   a. They saw it at the garlic festival last year.

   b. They wanted to contribute to the area they lived in.

   c. They had an old family formula.

6. Which types of garlic does Sandra Rappazini *not* mention as possible ingredients for the making of garlic wine?

   a. garlic essence

   b. garlic powder

   c. aged garlic

7. What do you know about Rappazini?

   a. She assembled a group called "The Vintage Four."

   b. Her friends laughed at her garlic wine.

   c. Her friends wrote a song for her.

8. According to the song, what will happen if you drink garlic wine?

   a. You'll forget what time it is.

   b. Your kisses will be sweet.

   c. You'll lose your friends.

PART 3

9. What suggestion would Rappazini make to people who couldn't get past their prejudice against garlic wine?

   a. She would convince them to try it with garlic-flavored food.

   b. She would convince them that it's a stuffy product.

   c. She would remind them that it's part of the California wine industry.

10. What does one taster say about the wine?

   a. It should be drunk with salad dressing.

   b. It should be used in salad dressing.

   c. It's similar to salad dressing.

11. Which of the following is a reaction of the wine tasters?

   a. It's dry.

   b. It's a great dinner wine.

   c. Their colleagues should try it.

7 LOOKING AT LANGUAGE

■ RHYME

Exercise 1

Listen to "The Garlic Song" and fill in the missing words.

1. You've heard about the _____

2. You shouldn't drink before its _____ .

(*continued on next page*)

3. And you've heard _____ the wine

4. That you _____ drink at any time.

5. But _____ us tell you now _____ a wine

6. That's raised _____ stink,

7. From a little _____ called Gilroy,

8. Where garlic _____ king.

9. It's Rappazini's garlic _____ .

10. Makes your kissin' sweet

11. _____ makes your breath mighty _____ .

12. It's Rappazini's garlic wine.

13. _____ it with a friend,

14. _____ have a mighty fine _____ .

Exercise 2

Read the following poem. It exemplifies the three types of rhyme commonly found in poetry and song.

> [1] I have met at close of *day*
> [2] Coming with vivid *faces*
> [3] From counter or desk among *grey*
> [4] Eighteenth-century *houses*.
> [5] I have passed with a nod of the *head*
> [6] Or polite meaningless *words*,
> [7] Or have lingered awhile and *said*
> [8] Polite meaningless *words*.
>
> (W. B. YEATS, FROM "EASTER," 1916)

"Perfect rhyme" is used when the endings (usually the last syllables) of two lines of verse have the same sound, but the words themselves are not the same, as in lines 1 and 3, or 5 and 7.

However, perfect rhyme is not always used. When "imperfect rhyme" is used, the endings of two lines of verse sound similar but, in fact, are not the same, as in lines 2 and 4.

In addition, you sometimes find the same word used at the end of two lines of verse, in which case a word "rhymes with itself," as in lines 6 and 8.

In jingles—short songs to advertise a product—rhyme is sometimes used to emphasize the message.

Read "The Garlic Song" again and answer the following questions:

1. Which two lines of verse illustrate perfect rhyme?

2. Which two lines of verse illustrate imperfect rhyme?

3. Which two lines of verse illustrate a word rhyming with itself?

Discuss the use of rhyme in your own language. Do these three examples of the use of rhyme also occur in your language?

8 FOLLOW-UP ACTIVITIES

DISCUSSION QUESTIONS

In groups, discuss your answers to the following questions:

1. Would people be willing to buy garlic wine in your country?

2. What is the best way to market a new product that might not be immediately popular with the public?

COMPOSITION TOPICS

Choose one of the following topics:

1. More and more Americans are drinking wine with dinner, as well as when they go out and socialize with friends. Do you agree with the drinking of alcohol in social situations? Write an essay in which you express your opinion.

(continued on next page)

2. How does advertising influence your decision to buy: in a positive or negative way? Write an essay in which you give examples to support your opinion.

■ DESIGN: A NEW PRODUCT

A. Taking Notes to Prepare

Listen to the interview again. Take notes on the design and marketing of the unusual product discussed in the interview. Key phrases and some examples have been provided for you.

By focusing on some of the considerations that go into developing a new product, you may be better able to create your own new product in the design exercise that follows.

THE DESIGN

Local resources used:

- *California garlic* _____

Description of the product:

_____

_____

_____

_____

_____

_____

_____

The label:

_____

_____

Research and development:

_____

_____

_____

_____

MARKETING

Taste trends and fashion:

* *Wine is fun*
_____

_____

Pricing:

_____

Promotion of product:

_____

B. Design

In the interview, you heard about a new wine. Why would anyone create garlic wine? This product was created because there was a natural resource available: garlic. And second, the producers knew that there was a market for American-made wine.

Work in groups. Think of an idea for an unusual product that would be fun to create. Prepare the design and marketing strategy for your product. In preparing your product, consider the following:

THE DESIGN

- The local resources available

- A description of your product (color, taste, etc.)

- Research and development

- The packaging

- The label (if any)

(continued on next page)

MARKETING

- Taste trends and fashion
- People who would buy this product
- The advertising strategy
- Pricing

Write a jingle or short advertisement for your product. Present your design, marketing plan, and jingle or short advertisement to the rest of the class.

"A Wine That's Raised Some Stink" was first broadcast on "Morning Edition," August 14, 1983. The interviewer is Lee Thornton.

DRIVE-IN SHOPPING

PREDICTING

From the title, discuss what you think the report is about.

2   THINK AHEAD

Work in groups. Read the following statements. Do you agree with them? See if everyone in your group has the same opinion.

1. It takes too much time to shop in today's busy world.

2. Catalog shopping is better than waiting in line in stores.

3. Computers have been the most important contribution to the workplace.

4. Many jobs still held by people could be more efficiently done by machines.

5. With the use of computers in many areas of work and at home, human relations have suffered.

3   VOCABULARY

Read the following sentences. The words in italics will help you understand the report. Try to determine the meaning of these words from the context of the sentences. Then write a synonym or your own definition of the words.

1. With the addition of computers in the office, many jobs that once took hours to finish are now being done in ***record time***.

   _____

2. According to some busy working women, grocery shopping is a ***hassle*** because it takes so much time, and it is so inconvenient.

   _____

3. Most working people ***are*** not really ***big on*** shopping for groceries when they get home from work. They'd rather relax, read the paper, or watch TV.

   _____

4. If a patient dies in a hospital, the body is usually sent to the hospital's ***mortuary*** before burial.

   _____

5. Some modern conveniences, such as drop-off laundromats, allow you to leave your work to be done by others while you ***go about your business*** shopping, working, or whatever.

   _____

6. In order to sell a new idea, advertising must have an original ***pitch*** to convince people to buy.

   _____

7. Because many people are starting to cook gourmet meals, many supermarkets now offer several ***fancy-grade*** food products.

   _____

8. Supermarkets often lose money with their ***perishable*** foods, such as fish and fruit, if they aren't purchased in a short time.

   _____

9. Prices aren't always ***comparable*** in different supermarkets. They're high in some and low in others, so it's necessary to shop wisely.

   _____

10. Many people have felt that banking with home computers is an idea ***whose time has really come***. It's a sign of the future.

    _____

11. If banking from home computers really ***catches on***, there may be more computer crimes.

    _____

12. McDonald's is an example of a successful American chain, because it has ***franchised*** throughout the United States, as well as in many other parts of the world.

    _____

Now try to match the words and expressions with a definition or synonym. Then compare your answers with those of another student. The first one has been done for you.

___h___ 1. record time

_____ 2. hassle

_____ 3. be big on something

_____ 4. mortuary

_____ 5. go about your business

_____ 6. pitch

_____ 7. fancy-grade

_____ 8. perishable

_____ 9. comparable

_____ 10. whose time has really come

_____ 11. catch on

_____ 12. franchise

a. aggressive sales talk

b. a room where dead bodies are kept

c. grant the right to sell services or products

d. easily spoiled

e. become popular

f. similar

g. special quality

h. the shortest time

i. continue doing your routine

j. like something a lot

k. annoying task

l. that fits today's needs

4   # TASK LISTENING

Listen to the report. Find the answer to the following question:

What is this grocery store's "reason for being"?

5   LISTENING FOR MAIN IDEAS

Listen to the report again. The report has been divided into four parts, each expressing a main idea. You will hear a beep at the end of each part. A word or phrase has been given for each part to help you focus on the main idea. Write the main idea in your own words. You should have four statements that make a summary of the report. Compare your summary with that of another student. Try to agree on the best expression of the main ideas. Part 1 has been done for you.

PART 1   Drive-in Supermarket

A new drive-in supermarket is saving time for shoppers in California.

PART 2   Successful Ideas

PART 3   Disadvantages

PART 4   Future

6   LISTENING FOR DETAILS

*Read the statements for Part 1. Then listen to Part 1 again and decide whether the statements are true or false. As you listen, write **T** or **F** next to each statement. Compare your answers with those of another student. If you disagree, listen to Part 1 again.*

PART 1

_____ 1. In Los Angeles, 1,200 people shop at the same time.

_____ 2. A new supermarket can accommodate 300 cars an hour.

_____ 3. In this supermarket, shopping takes six minutes.

_____ 4. One woman usually waits in line for a couple of hours at a regular grocery store.

_____ 5. She doesn't like to shop.

Repeat the same procedure for Parts 2–4.

PART 2

_____ 6. This new supermarket is near two freeways.

_____ 7. The supermarket offers lots of parking.

_____ 8. Drive-through chapels and mortuaries have been successful throughout the United States.

_____ 9. There are 4,000 items to buy in this supermarket.

_____ 10. Customers mail in their grocery lists.

_____ 11. Then the computer packs the bags.

_____ 12. The shopper only has to load the groceries into the car.

PART 3

_____ 13. It takes the supermarket two minutes to find your order.

_____ 14. It's sometimes hard to find a parking space.

_____ 15. With this shopping, you have to buy high-quality food.

_____ 16. People sometimes complain about the freshness of the food.

_____ 17. Prices are a bit higher in this store.

_____ 18. One woman complained about the number of people who shop in grocery stores.

PART 4

_____ 19. This supermarket is not doing as well as expected.

_____ 20. This supermarket is being franchised throughout the country.

_____ 21. Some people order their groceries from home computers.

_____ 22. Some people order their groceries while watching TV.

7   LOOKING AT LANGUAGE

▣ VERBS TO DESCRIBE THE SENSES

Exercise 1

Listen to the following segment of the report. It describes how people "test" the freshness of food in supermarkets.

> There are disadvantages to this fast-lane grocery shopping.
> You can't stop and **sniff** the fish or **squeeze** the melon.

Certain verbs are used to describe the way we perceive things through our senses. The two verbs from the example have been categorized under one of the five senses. We **sniff** fish in order to smell its freshness, and we **squeeze** a melon in order to touch it.

(continued on next page)

Work with another student. Discuss the meaning of the verbs listed below. Use your dictionary to help you. Then write the verbs on the chart under the appropriate heading. Some verbs may fit into more than one category.

overhear	grasp	lick	stare
spot	catch sight of	savor	pinch
rub	fondle	eavesdrop	take a whiff
inhale	handle	witness	perceive
sip	notice	glimpse	stroke

	Taste	Smell	Touch	Sight	Hearing
		sniff	squeeze		

Exercise 2

Describe one of the following experiences:

- Trying a new food for the first time

- Witnessing an unexpected event

- Touching something you were not able to see

Try to use some of the verbs from your chart.

8 FOLLOW-UP ACTIVITIES

■ DISCUSSION QUESTIONS

In groups, discuss your answers to the following questions:

1. Would you shop at a drive-in supermarket if there were one in your hometown? Why or why not?

2. Discuss jobs that take less time today with the help of machines. Do you feel that putting machines in the workplace has done more to help workers save time, or do you feel more time is wasted in training people to deal with machines?

■ COMPOSITION TOPICS

Choose one of the following topics:

1. Write an essay describing the effects that machines and computers have had on society today. Include your view of technological progress.

2. Write an essay in which you describe a familiar place that no longer looks or functions the way it used to, because of modern technology: the use of modern machines, computers, automation, etc. Include your view of these changes.

■ DESIGN: A DRIVE-IN OF THE FUTURE

A. Taking Notes to Prepare

Listen to the interview again. Take notes on the drive-in supermarket described in the report. Key phrases and an example have been provided for you.

By focusing on the considerations that go into the design of the California drive-in supermarket, you may be better able to create your own drive-through service in the design exercise that follows.

The service:

drive-in supermarket
_____

The location:

_____

The number of cars that can be accommodated:

_____

The ordering procedure:

_____

_____

_____

The use of computers:

_____

_____

_____

The disadvantages to consider:

_____

_____

The prices:

_____

B. Design

In this interview, you heard about drive-through conveniences such as grocery stores, banks, and even mortuaries and chapels.

Work in groups. Consider the amount of time it takes to obtain services in today's busy world. What type of service might be obtained more easily if you could drive through? Design a drive-in of the future. In planning, consider the following:

- The name of your drive-in

- The service(s)

- The location

- The number of cars accommodated in an hour

- The use or nonuse of computers as part of the service

- The ordering procedure

- The prices

Write a description of your drive-in, and present it to the rest of the class.

"Drive-in Shopping" was first broadcast on "All Things Considered," July 20, 1983. The reporter is America Rodriguez.

Is It a Sculpture, Or Is It Food?

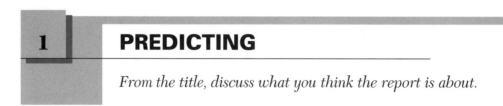

1   **PREDICTING**

From the title, discuss what you think the report is about.

2   THINK AHEAD

In groups, discuss your answers to the following questions:

1. What do you know about genetic engineering? In what areas of life is it being used today?

2. In buying fruits and vegetables, which is more important: taste, texture, color, nutritional value, price, or shelf life? Why?

3. Have you ever eaten food that was genetically engineered? What did it look like? What did it taste like?

4. What fears might genetic engineering provoke in people?

3   VOCABULARY

Read the text. The words in italics will help you understand the interview. Try to determine the meaning of these words. Then match the words with their definitions or synonyms in the list at the end of the text. Write the number of each word next to its definition or synonym. The first one has been done for you.

Experiments in genetic engineering have created important ***breakthroughs*** in many areas; they have led to cures for many diseases, the control of insect populations, and the improvement of food production. However, most of these experiments are not ***foolproof***; no one knows for sure what negative consequences they could have.

People often ***poke fun at*** progress, possibly because technology often presents new problems as it attempts to solve old ones. Imagine what might happen to genes that have been genetically engineered in scientists' laboratories once they are released into the environment. The

ramifications of introducing these genes could be terrifying: Some talk
of the creation of human monsters, or Frankensteins. In fact, there
already exists genetically manipulated food that has been called
"Frankenfood" by some.

Whether or not the fear of science-fiction food is realistic, genetically
engineered food has received a great deal of attention recently because
many of these food products are now on the market. For example, gene-
spliced foods have been developed to improve the color, taste, and shelf
life of fruits and vegetables. Some people are concerned that these foods
don't have the same taste or that they may cause people to become sick.
For example, *trout* genes are now used to produce longer-lasting
tomatoes. Yet, people who have *allergies* to fish may become ill from
eating these tomatoes, if the trout gene has not been sufficiently
sublimated in the gene-splicing process. Restaurant owners, as well as
others who work with food, have started to *boycott* these foods to show
their disagreement with this type of food production.

On the other hand, many people recognize that genetically
manipulated food can bring many benefits to our lives. It could increase
food production throughout the world and begin to solve the hunger
problem. It could improve the taste and life of food. Genetically
engineered food could also end our dependence on pesticides to protect
crops; if fewer pesticides were used, the problem of *pesticide residue* in

food could be reduced. Finally, these foods could provide a ***boon*** to the
food industry, which could help the general economy.

Most people will agree that more information is needed before we
can be sure whether genetically engineered products will improve our
lives. We need to weigh the advantages with the disadvantages, as well as
consider the dangers, before we make further commitments to
experimenting in this area.

_____ rapid increase or expansion	_____ incapable of error; always effective
_____ sensitivity to things, such as particular foods	__1__ major achievements
_____ weakened	_____ whatever remains after treatment used to destroy insects
_____ joined end to end	
_____ a freshwater fish	_____ refuse to use or buy goods, as a form of protest
_____ consequences	_____ make fun of

---

4 # TASK LISTENING

Listen to the interview. Find the answer to the following question:

> Is Joyce Goldstein more in favor of or more against
> genetically engineered food?

5 | LISTENING FOR MAIN IDEAS

Listen to the interview again. The interview has been divided into four parts, each expressing a main idea. You will hear a beep at the end of each part. A word or phrase has been given for each part to help you focus on the main idea. Write the main idea in your own words. You should have four statements that make a summary of the interview. Compare your summary with that of another student. Try to agree on the best expression of the main ideas. Part 1 has been done for you.

PART 1   boycott

Chefs from around the country have boycotted genetically engineered food.

PART 2   the tomato

_____

PART 3   lack of information

_____

PART 4   right to know

_____

6 | LISTENING FOR DETAILS

*Read the statements for Part 1. Then listen to Part 1 again and decide whether the statements are true or false. As you listen, write **T** or **F** next to each statement. Compare your answers with those of another student. If you disagree, listen again to Part 1.*

PART 1

_____ 1. Genetically designed tomatoes are now* available in the supermarket.

_____ 2. Genetically engineered cheese can now be purchased.

* at the time the interview was recorded

_____ 3. World hunger may be helped with genetically engineered food.

_____ 4. Last week* 1,000 chefs decided not to serve genetically engineered food.

_____ 5. Special labeling is required for genetically engineered food.

_____ 6. Goldstein owns a restaurant in San Francisco.

Repeat the same procedure for Parts 2–4.

PART 2

Goldstein believes . . .

_____ 7. the genetically engineered tomato is being produced for flavor.

_____ 8. the use of fish genes in tomatoes is a good idea.

_____ 9. these foods should be thoroughly tested and labeled before they are sold.

PART 3

According to Goldstein . . .

_____ 10. "progress" is our enemy.

_____ 11. the methods of the old days were better than those today.

_____ 12. genetically bred roses are very beautiful and smell good.

_____ 13. restaurants shouldn't serve genetically engineered food until it is tested.

_____ 14. we should worry about corporate profit.

_____ 15. people who don't understand her boycott wouldn't be welcome to eat in her restaurant.

_____ 16. The Food and Drug Administration** does a good job of regulating these foods.

* at the time the interview was recorded
**government organization that regulates the sale and use of food and drugs

PART 4

According to Goldstein . . .

_____ 17. pesticide residue in foods is a problem.

_____ 18. genetic manipulation of foods to reduce their dependence on pesticides is a good thing.

_____ 19. the crossing of trout with tomatoes is a good thing.

_____ 20. genetic experimentation should work on improving the taste of foods.

_____ 21. what is good for agribusiness is generally good for the consumer.

_____ 22. consumers are given the information they need in purchasing food.

7   LOOKING AT LANGUAGE

ADJECTIVE CLAUSES

The use of adjective clauses can make language sound more sophisticated in both writing and speaking. Rather than expressing an idea in two simple sentences that repeat the same noun, you can replace the noun in one sentence with a relative pronoun (*who, which, that*). This changes two simple sentences into one more-complex sentence, as in the following example:

> In the near future, you might be able to buy a **tomato** in the supermarket.

> The **tomato** has been genetically designed and engineered.

Instead of repeating the noun *tomato* two times, the interviewer uses an adjective clause:

> In the near future, you might be able to buy a tomato in the supermarket **that has been genetically designed and engineered.**

Exercise

Listen to the beginning of the introduction to the interview. Underline all the adjective clauses. Circle the relative pronouns, and draw arrows to the nouns they describe. The first one has been done for you.

In the near future, you might be able to buy a tomato in the supermarket (that) has been genetically designed and engineered, a tomato that would stay ripe much longer, strawberries that are not so fragile in freezing temperatures, vegetable oil that's lower in fat. Already on the market: a gene-spliced product that's used in cheese making. There are impressive claims being made for genetic manipulation of food, including production increases that could help alleviate world hunger. But there's also concern, and indeed some fear, about the use of gene-splicing techniques . . . .

8   FOLLOW-UP ACTIVITIES

▦ DISCUSSION QUESTIONS

In groups, discuss your answers to the following questions:

1. Should genetically engineered food be boycotted by restaurant owners?

2. Should the Food and Drug Administration require special labeling for genetically engineered foods?

3. Some people have called genetically engineered food "science-fiction food" or even "Frankenfood." Do you think human beings' manipulation of nature benefits or harms society? Where do you stand on the issue of scientific progress?

■ COMPOSITION TOPICS

Choose one of the following topics:

1. Scientists who experiment with genes have sometimes been accused of "playing God." Do you agree with this accusation? Write an essay in which you express your opinion.

2. Write an essay in which you discuss the advantages and disadvantages of producing genetically engineered foods. How can this experimentation help the world, and how might it harm the world? Draw your own conclusions as to whether this experimentation should be continued or curtailed.

■ VALUES CLARIFICATION: GENETIC EXPERIMENTATION

A. Taking Notes to Prepare

Listen to the interview again. Take notes on the benefits and disadvantages of genetic engineering. Key phrases and some examples have been provided for you.

By focusing on Goldstein's concerns about genetically engineered food, you may be better able to see the pros and cons of genetic engineering in other areas as well. Use your notes to help you in the ***values clarification*** exercise that follows.

Benefits of genetic engineering:
- *longer-life tomato*
- *less fragile strawberries*

Disadvantages of genetic engineering:

- *gene-splicing techniques not clear*
- *no special labeling for such food*

B. Values Clarification

Work in groups. Read the following proposals for experiments involving genetic engineering. Note the public's concern about the danger of each experiment.

Decide which experiments should be conducted. Rank these choices from the one you think is the most important (number 1) to the one you think is the least important (number 5) for improving today's world.

Try to reach a group consensus.

_____ CHARACTER TRAIT SELECTION

These experiments would attempt to transfer genes to embryos and develop the cloning process. By selecting and transferring special genes to animals, farmers could create larger and stronger livestock. These experiments could develop a system for human gene selection. Parents would be able to choose the genetic traits of their children.

Public concern: Choosing character traits is not ethical. It is cruel to animals to use them for this experimentation.

_____ CURE FOR DISEASES

These experiments would develop a cure for diseases by manipulating genes in humans. Scientists hope to clone virus genes in order to treat patients and eventually develop a cure for the disease.

Public concern: The treatment could affect normal cells in the body and hurt the patient. Side effects from these drugs might be passed on to future generations.

(continued on next page)

_____ INCREASE OF WORLD FOOD SUPPLY

These experiments would field-test genetically engineered bacteria on crops to help control frost damage. Experimental pesticides would also be developed through genetic engineering to use in farming. These experiments would also improve the shelf life of fruits and vegetables. More food could be produced for Third World countries.

Public concern: The experimentation causes gene mutation that could be irreversible. No one is really sure what effect this field testing would have on the environment. Introducing new organisms into the earth's environment could be damaging. The crossing of food genes could result in allergies that people are unaware of.

_____ MILITARY DEVELOPMENT

These experiments would attempt to create biological weapons by means of gene splicing and recombining DNA.* Some countries are already working on these experiments and could take a lead in military power with these new weapons.

Public concern: The development of these weapons could increase the possibilities of biological warfare.

_____ FERTILITY REGULATION

These experiments would attempt to clone hormones to regulate fertility in humans. Experiments would also develop techniques for artificial insemination and embryo transfer.

Public concern: The hormones could get out of control and a person might become "too fertile," conceiving more children than desired. Fertilization experiments tamper with nature.

°DNA: **D**eoxyribo**n**ucleic **a**cid—acid located in the nucleus of a cell that carries the genetic information.

"Is It A Sculpture, or Is It Food?" was first broadcast on "All Things Considered," August 3, 1992. The interviewer is Noah Adams.

GANG VIOLENCE

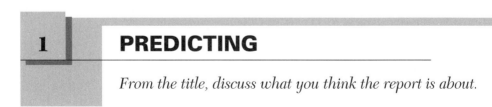

1 **PREDICTING**

From the title, discuss what you think the report is about.

THINK AHEAD

In groups, discuss your answers to the following questions:

1. Do gangs exist in your country?

2. What methods are used to control teenage criminals in your country?

3. Why do you think teenagers in the United States join gangs?

VOCABULARY

Read the following sentences. The words in italics will help you understand the interview. Try to determine the meaning of these words from the context of the sentences. Then write a synonym or your own definition of the words.

1. Gangs won't normally allow girls to join them, so they tend to be ***exclusively*** male.

   _____

2. Some boys who join gangs are ***cowards*** because they are afraid to commit a crime by themselves.

   _____

3. People will instinctively ***duck*** and cover themselves when a gun is fired in their direction.

   _____

4. Gang members will sometimes identify with a ***pimp***, not because he works with prostitutes, but because he makes a lot of money.

   _____

5. In order to identify which gang a member belongs to, certain signals are used to represent his ***affiliation***.

   _____

6. Gangs use a much more severe method of fighting than the traditional **punch** in the nose.

   _____

7. Gang members are considered to be insensitive because they feel so little **remorse** after they've hurt someone.

   _____

8. The money brought in from crime is often the only source of **livelihood** for gang members.

   _____

9. People living in cities are forming more and more **block clubs** to provide protection for their communities.

   _____

10. One of the least dangerous crimes committed by gangs is the drawing of **graffiti** on public property.

    _____

Now try to match the words with a definition or synonym. Then compare your answers with those of another student. The first one has been done for you.

_d_ 1. exclusively	a. a way to earn money
___ 2. coward	b. a neighborhood group
___ 3. duck	c. a man who sells sex
___ 4. pimp	d. only
___ 5. affiliation	e. bend down quickly to avoid being hit
___ 6. punch	f. association
___ 7. remorse	g. writing on a wall, bus, or subway car, etc.
___ 8. livelihood	h. a person who runs away from danger
___ 9. block club	i. a blow with the fist of a hand
___ 10. graffiti	j. regret for wrongdoing

4   TASK LISTENING

Listen to the interview. Find the answer to the following question:

> Do gang members kill people?

5   LISTENING FOR MAIN IDEAS

Listen to the interview again. The interview has been divided into five parts, each expressing a main idea. You will hear a beep at the end of each part. Answer the question for each part in a complete sentence. You should have five statements that make a summary of the interview. Compare your summary with that of another student.

PART 1   Where is there a large number of gangs in the United States?

_____

_____

PART 2   How do gangs fight?

_____

_____

PART 3   Why do kids join gangs?

_____

PART 4   How do gangs identify themselves to each other?

_____

_____

PART 5   What solution does Bill Recktenwald propose for controlling gang violence?

_____

_____

6 | **LISTENING FOR DETAILS**

*Read the statements for Part 1. Then listen to Part 1 again and decide whether the statements are true or false. As you listen, write **T** or **F** next to each statement. Compare your answers with those of another student. If you disagree, listen to Part 1 again.*

PART 1

_____ 1. In 1983, there were at least seventy-five gang murders in Chicago.

_____ 2. Ten percent of Chicago's murders are gang murders.

_____ 3. Chicago has fewer than 100 gangs.

_____ 4. Each gang has about 4,000 members.

_____ 5. Gang members are generally less than twenty years old.

Repeat the same procedure for Parts 2–5.

PART 2

Gang members . . .

_____ 6. are male.

_____ 7. are independent.

_____ 8. fight alone.

_____ 9. shoot at people.

_____ 10. kill innocent people.

PART 3

People join gangs because . . .

_____ 11. they have a strong identity.

_____ 12. gangs make them feel big.

(continued on next page)

_____ 13. pimps and drug dealers are in gangs.

_____ 14. they want to make money.

_____ 15. they can use drugs and narcotics.

PART 4

Innocent people are victimized because . . .

_____ 16. hand signals are not understood.

_____ 17. they punch the wrong people in the nose.

_____ 18. gangs are insensitive to someone getting killed.

PART 5

Recktenwald says gangs should be controlled by . . .

_____ 19. parents.

_____ 20. schools.

_____ 21. the community.

_____ 22. neighborhood block clubs.

7   LOOKING AT LANGUAGE

■ TONE OF VOICE

Exercise 1

Listen to the following segment of the interview. Focus on the tone of voice the interviewer uses as she responds to Bill Recktenwald.

RECKTENWALD:

This is, surprisingly enough, an area that I think we can control much easier than many of our problems in society. We're talking about generally here a lack of control of young people by their parents. So, you control . . . you know, you get parents to control their kids.

INTERVIEWER:

But, Bill, you're talking about, probably in most cases, families that are very fragile or nonexistent. That's why these kids are in this situation. I mean, you can't just press a button and say, "Well, families, be responsible."

What tone of voice does the interviewer use when she reacts by saying "But, Bill"? Does her voice sound surprised, angry, annoyed? How do you think she feels about his suggestion that parents should control kids?

A great deal is communicated through the tone of voice in English. How does the interviewer's response change the direction of the interview? What does Recktenwald begin to focus on as a result of her response? What do you think he would have talked about if the interviewer had not responded the way she did?

Exercise 2

Work in pairs. Practice using tone of voice to express emotion. Read the following short dialogues aloud. Student A reads the first statement. Student B reads the response, expressing the first emotion indicated in parentheses. Then Student B reads the response again, using a different tone of voice to express the other emotion indicated. Change roles so that each student has an opportunity to read the responses two times.

1. STUDENT A:
   In 1983, 10 percent of the murders in Chicago were attributed to street-gang violence.

   STUDENT B:
   Where did you get that information? (disbelief/interest)

2. STUDENT A:
   Believe it or not, gang members are usually cowards.

   STUDENT B:
   I find that hard to believe. (sarcasm/doubt)

3. STUDENT A:
   Sometimes innocent victims get killed when gangs fight in the street.

   STUDENT B:
   Something should be done. (concern/anger)

(continued on next page)

4. **STUDENT A:**
   The reason kids join gangs is that there is a lack of control by their parents.

   STUDENT B:
   But these kids don't usually have families. (annoyance/sadness)

5. **STUDENT A:**
   If the community works together, they can push the gangs out.

   STUDENT B:
   What can the community do? (doubt/interest)

8 FOLLOW-UP ACTIVITIES

■ DISCUSSION QUESTIONS

In groups, discuss your answers to the following questions:

1. Do you agree with Recktenwald that the community should control gangs? To what extent should people watch the activities of others?

2. What should the punishment be for minors (kids under the age of twenty-one) when they kill innocent people?

■ COMPOSITION TOPICS

Choose one of the following topics:

1. Write a letter to the editor of your local newspaper, making the point that you are unhappy about street-gang violence in your neighborhood. Explain your reasons clearly, giving examples of gang incidents that you know about. Ask the community to form a block club to support the cause of fighting gang violence.

2. People say society has gone wrong by producing youngsters who commit serious crimes. Do you agree? Write an essay in which you state your opinion, and define the best way to treat the problem.

■ ROLE PLAY: WITNESS TO A CRIME

A. Taking Notes to Prepare

Listen to the interview again. Take notes on what gangs are like and what neighborhood watch clubs can do. Key phrases and some examples have been provided for you.

By reviewing some of the details that have been described in the interview, you may have a better background for preparing the **role play** that follows.

Description of gangs:

- *under age 20*
- *individuals afraid to stand alone*

_____

_____

_____

_____

_____

Reason for gangs:

_____

_____

_____

_____

Gang rituals:

_____

_____

_____

_____

(continued on next page)

What neighborhood watch clubs can do:

_____

_____

_____

_____

_____

B. Role Play

For this role play, the class is divided into two groups. Two students will prepare the witnesses' stories. The others will prepare the interrogation by the police. Read the situation, choose roles, and, after a fifteen-minute preparation, begin the interrogation of witnesses to a crime.

THE SITUATION

Last night, at 10:30 P.M., two members of a neighborhood block club witnessed a theft. They saw two boys break into a car that was parked in the neighborhood. The boys broke the side window and ran off with the car's radio and tape deck.

The police were notified by the witnesses. By the time they got to the scene of the crime, the boys were gone.

Two teenage boys, who seem to fit the description given by the witnesses, were found loitering on a corner in the neighborhood at 11:30 P.M. They have been brought to the station.

However, members of the neighborhood watch club have been known to accuse the wrong people of street crimes, since they are so concerned about the protection of their neighborhood. Because the police are not sure whether these boys are the ones the witnesses really saw, they have separated the two witnesses to hear each one give his or her own version of the story. The witnesses' testimony will certainly have a great influence on the future of these two young boys.

THE ROLES

THE WITNESSES

You are witnesses to the crime. You will prepare a detailed account of what happened. Explain what you were doing when you witnessed the crime and what you saw. You should be able to explain:

- Where you were
- Who you were with
- What the boys were doing
- What the boys looked like, etc.

THE POLICE

You will prepare questions to ask the witnesses. For example:

- Where were you?
- Who were you with?
- What time was it?
- What did you see?
- Why were you watching the street corner?
- How were the boys dressed?

INTERROGATION PROCEDURE

1. The police divide into two groups. One group interrogates one witness while the other interrogates the second. These interrogations last three minutes.

2. Next, each witness is interrogated by the other group of police for another three minutes. If the police find discrepancies in the two witnesses' stories, the boys will be released. If the stories are similar, they will be accused of being guilty of the crime.

3. Each group of police explains the inconsistencies, if any, that they were able to find in the two versions. They then decide on their verdict.

"Gang Violence" was first broadcast on "All Things Considered," January 9, 1984. The interviewer is Nina Totenberg.

Create Controversy to Generate Publicity

6

UNITED COLORS OF BENETTON.

---

1 ## PREDICTING

From the title, discuss what you think the interview is about.

2 THINK AHEAD

In groups, discuss your answers to the following questions:

1. What makes an ad successful? Give examples to explain your answer.

2. Can you think of any companies that have used controversial advertising? What was different about their ads? What reactions did they get from the public?

3. In your opinion, should companies use advertising to promote certain values?

3 VOCABULARY

Read the following sentences. The words in italics will help you understand the interview. Try to determine the meaning of these words from the context of the sentences. Then write a synonym or your own definition of the words.

1. The Benetton ad has been ***controversial*** because some people see it as a way to improve race relations, while others see it only as a way to promote the company's business.

   _____

2. One of the most important decisions a company must make is how to ***depict*** the company in its advertisements: through photographs, graphic design, illustrations, or other means.

   _____

3. In Catholic schools, ***nuns*** are often classroom teachers.

   _____

4. Bright colors usually ***enhance*** the visual appeal of an advertisement.

   _____

5. Choosing the best way to increase ***consumer exposure*** to a new product is key to successful advertising.

   _____

(continued on next page)

6. Magazines are a "natural **habitat**" for ads; most of the space in magazines is reserved for advertising in order to generate revenues.

———————————————————————————————

7. An unborn baby is attached to its mother by the **umbilicus**, which is cut when the baby is born.

———————————————————————————————

8. Advertisers will sometimes take extreme measures to create an **arresting** ad, one that is sure to get the public's attention.

———————————————————————————————

9. It's best not to ask people how their marriage is going if they are **touchy** about discussing their personal lives.

———————————————————————————————

10. Advertising is generally used to attract people to a product, not to **tick** them **off** or get them upset about an issue.

———————————————————————————————

11. Focusing on world issues rather than on the cost of a product is a **cunning** method of advertising.

———————————————————————————————

12. When people need to save money, the **rational** approach is to shop less frequently.

———————————————————————————————

Now try to match the words with a definition or synonym. The first one has been done for you.

_k_   1. controversial

_____ 2. depict

_____ 3. nuns

_____ 4. enhance

_____ 5. consumer exposure

_____ 6. habitat

a. overly sensitive

b. describe; represent in a picture or words

c. sneaky; sly

d. make angry

e. reasonable; logical

_____ 7. umbilicus

_____ 8. arresting

_____ 9. touchy

_____ 10. tick off

_____ 11. cunning

_____ 12. rational

f. contact with people who will buy the product

g. cord connecting a fetus to the mother

h. place where something lives or exists; a place where something is usually found

i. striking; holding the attention of someone

j. women who live life in the service of God

k. creating argument

l. add to; increase in beauty or value

4 TASK LISTENING

Listen to the interview. Find the answer to the following question:

How much does a cotton T-shirt cost at Benetton?

5 LISTENING FOR MAIN IDEAS

Listen to the interview again. The interview has been divided into four parts, each expressing a main idea. You will hear a beep at the end of each part. Answer the question for each part in a complete sentence. You should have four statements that make a summary of the report. Compare your summary with that of another student.

PART 1   What has Benetton done that has caused controversy?

_____

PART 2   How do the Benetton ads help the company?

_____

(continued on next page)

PART 3 How do the views of the newborn-baby ad differ?

_____

PART 4 According to Bob Garfield, what two purposes do these ads have?

_____

6 | LISTENING FOR DETAILS

Read the questions for Part 1. Then listen to Part 1 again. As you listen, circle the best answer. Compare your answers with those of another student. If you disagree, listen to Part 1 again.

PART 1

1. Which of the following is *not* true about the magazine advertising business?

    a. The magazine business is doing very well.

    b. Magazines are not publishing as many ads.

    c. Magazines are turning down controversial ads.

2. Which of the following does *not* describe one of the Benetton ads?

    a. a nun kissing a priest

    b. a newborn baby

    c. a black boy kissing a blonde girl

3. Why is Garfield being interviewed?

    a. He is an advertising critic for a magazine.

    b. He works for the Benetton company.

    c. He called to express his opinions.

Repeat the same procedure for Parts 2–4.

PART 2

4. Why does Garfield think Benetton has produced these ads?

   a. to put Garfield on the radio for an interview

   b. to generate publicity

   c. to place Benetton ads into a new habitat

5. How does Garfield think people probably react when they see the ad with the picture of the newborn baby?

   a. casually

   b. not seriously

   c. angrily

PART 3

6. Which description would Garfield most likely use to describe the picture of the newborn baby?

   a. arresting

   b. disgusting

   c. magnificent

7. Why does Garfield talk about using a picture of a large intestine?

   a. He thinks it is more natural than that of the newborn baby.

   b. He would like to see one used in a fashion magazine.

   c. He tries to show us that the Benetton ads have gone too far.

PART 4

8. Which magazine published the ad with the newborn baby?

   a. *Essence* magazine

   b. *Self* magazine

   c. *Cosmopolitan* magazine

(continued on next page)

9. How does the interviewer react to the magazines?

    a. She is surprised they didn't publish the ads.

    b. She objects to their double-page ads.

    c. She thinks they are too skinny.

10. What did Benetton expect to happen with these ads?

    a. It expected most magazines to publish them.

    b. It expected the picture of the newborn baby to become popular.

    c. It wanted to get its customers angry.

11. Why does Garfield think Benetton's advertising is cunning?

    a. It causes the company to actually lose publicity.

    b. It's a form of distraction marketing.

    c. It helps consumers pay attention to prices.

12. What is Garfield's opinion about Benetton pricing?

    a. It's rational.

    b. Their cotton T-shirts are reasonably priced.

    c. Their cardigan sweaters are too expensive.

7   LOOKING AT LANGUAGE

■ DESCRIPTIVE ADJECTIVES

Many descriptive adjectives were used in this discussion of Benetton's ads. Work in groups. Listen again to the following comments that were made in the interview. Focus on the italicized words.

1. INTERVIEWER:
    I think that if you . . . uh . . . if you were paging through a magazine and you saw this picture, you would stop cold, even if you'd never heard of the ad or Benetton, because it is such an ***arresting*** picture, this baby.

2. GARFIELD:

    Well, it is that, . . . uh, arresting, some would say ***disgusting***, . . . And I suppose the Benetton people would say that it's ***magnificent*** and ***natural***.

3. GARFIELD:

    It's really very ***cunning*** advertising, Linda, for a lot of reasons.

4. GARFIELD:

    It's ***distracting***, because, rather than focus on trying to come up with some sort of rational benefit for buying a forty-nine dollar cotton T-shirt, which Benetton knows is not a rational kind of consumer behavior, they're kind of playing a little three-card monte in creating a distraction over here so you won't pay attention to the facts of the matter over on the other side, the facts of the matter being that a $119 cardigan sweater is not a particularly good buy.

Exercise

Create descriptors for ads and types of advertising. Write as many words as you can think of that have similar meaning to each adjective. Create lists of related words, and discuss any differences among the words you have included in each list.

arresting: _____

disgusting: _____

magnificent: _____

natural: _____

cunning: _____

distracting: _____

8   FOLLOW-UP ACTIVITIES

▨ DISCUSSION QUESTIONS

In groups, discuss your answers to the following questions:

1. Do you agree with Garfield's comment that Benetton's ads are an example of "distraction marketing"? Is the purpose of these ads to distract customers from the high prices of Benetton clothing?

2. Many companies give some of their profits to charity. Benetton has remarked that this money can often disappear without educating people, without even reaching people. They claim that their ads sometimes contribute more, by creating awareness. Do you agree or disagree?

▨ COMPOSITION TOPICS

Choose one of the following topics:

1. Benetton's photographer, Oliviero Toscani, has said:

   Advertising is not just about the selling of a product. It has an equal social obligation to do something more.

   The director of a Chicago advertising firm has said:

   Advertising should sell the product it's designed to sell and not be social commentary.

   Which of the two statements do you agree with? Write an essay in which you discuss your opinion.

2. One of Benetton's most controversial ads depicted a man in bed, dying of AIDS, surrounded by his family. The photograph had first appeared as an editorial photograph in *Life* magazine.

   Some people criticized this ad because they felt that AIDS was being exploited to sell a product. Benetton said that their advertisment says something that is real about things that exist, problems that touch everybody.

Where do you draw the line in the use of photography for advertising a product? Write an essay in which you discuss your ideas. Use examples to support your opinion.

■ VALUES CLARIFICATION: MAGAZINE ADVERTISEMENTS

A. Taking Notes to Prepare

Listen to the interview again. Take notes on Benetton's advertising and the effect it has had on the public. Key phrases and some examples have been provided for you.

By focusing on Benetton's purpose behind its ads, the public reaction to these ads, and other magazines' publishing decisions, you may be better able to clarify your values in the exercise that follows.

Benetton's purpose behind the ads:
  • *create controversy and generate publicity*
  _____
  _____
  _____
  _____
  _____

Public reaction to the ads:
  • *look at them seriously*
  _____
  _____
  _____
  _____
  _____

(continued on next page)

Other magazines' publishing decisions for Benetton ads:

- *Essence and Child: rejected the ad with the children*

B. Values Clarification

Imagine that you are the advertising team of *Life* magazine. You have traditionally carried advertisements for clothing manufacturers, including Benetton. In fact, Benetton ads bring a lot of money to your magazine.

There has been much controversy over Benetton's ads, and some magazines have refused to run them. You must decide which Benetton ads, if any, you will run in your magazine.

Work in groups. Examine the following proposed ads (pages 64–66). Use adjectives from Section 7 to describe your reactions to the ads. Decide which of the ads you will consider publishing. Rank your choices in order of "most favorable" (number 1) to "least favorable" (number 6). Try to reach a group consensus.

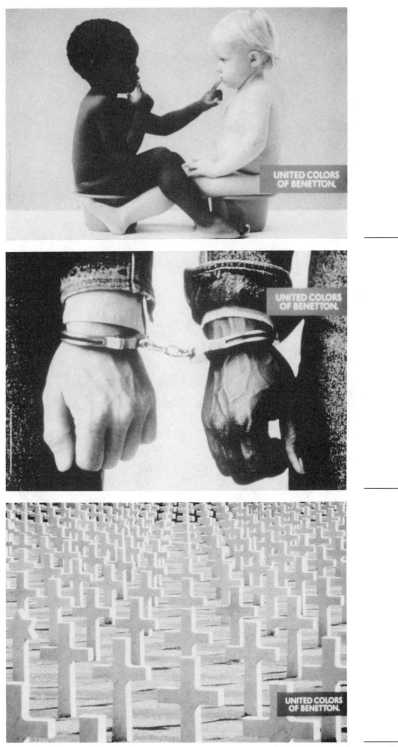

(continued on next page)

"Create Controversy to Generate Publicity" was first broadcast on "All Things Considered," September 30, 1991. The interviewer is Linda Wertheimer.

WOMEN CAUGHT IN THE MIDDLE OF TWO GENERATIONS

 1 ## PREDICTING

From the title, discuss what you think the interview is about.

THINK AHEAD

In groups, discuss your answers to the following questions:

1. Do all the members of a family live together in your country? Do children leave home at a certain age, or do they continue to live with their parents when they get married and have children?

2. What happens to old people as they begin to require care in your country? Do their children or friends take care of them, or do they live in nursing homes*?

3. Is the attitude toward older adults in America different from that in your own country?

VOCABULARY

Read the text. The words in italics will help you understand the report. Try to determine the meaning of these words. Then match the words with their definitions or synonyms in the list at the end of the text. Write the number of each word next to its definition or synonym. The first one has been done for you.

People are living longer in the United States. As a result, more and more middle-aged adults are becoming caretakers of their aging parents. When their parents can no longer care for themselves, these adults stay at home to care for them in much the same way they cared for their own children.

Playing the role of "parent-***sitter***" is quite difficult and frustrating. For example, an aging parent may become ***blind***. No longer able to see, the old person needs his or her children to perform many everyday jobs.

---

* *nursing home:* a private hospital where sick or old people live and are cared for by nurses and doctors

Another example is the parent who becomes ***brain-damaged*** during the aging process. Natural roles are then reversed, as children are forced to care for their parents as if their parents were children.

This change of roles is often quite difficult for the middle-aged child. As a dependent parent becomes a constant ***companion*** of his or her middle-aged child, family relationships sometimes suffer a great ***strain***. With a dependent parent living in the house, a family may feel a lack of ***privacy*** and a sense of no longer being able to live a normal life. When children of dependent parents feel ***trapped*** in this situation, they often decide to ***transplant*** their aging parent to a nursing home, where proper care and attention can be given. This allows the children to return to a normal family life.

The decision to put a parent in a nursing home is not always a comfortable one for children. They are often left with a feeling of ***shame*** if they choose to no longer care for their own parents. They feel that it is a child's ***duty*** to meet the needs of a parent, yet they desperately want their independence and privacy. The choice of caring for aging parents at home or putting them in nursing homes is becoming a difficult one for many Americans.

_____ person who goes everywhere with you

_____ unable to see

_____ caught

_____ loss of self-respect

_____ state of being alone and undisturbed

_____ obligation

_____ having illness affecting the brain

_____ tension; emotional pressures

_____ move

__1__ person paid to care for someone else, usually children

4   TASK LISTENING

Listen to the report. Find the answer to the following question:

Who often takes care of aging parents in the United States?

5   LISTENING FOR MAIN IDEAS

Listen to the report again. The report has been divided into five parts, each expressing a main idea. You will hear a beep at the end of each part. A word or phrase has been given for each part to help you focus on the main idea. Write the main idea in your own words. You should have five statements that make a summary of the report. Compare your summary with that of another student. Try to agree on the best expression of the main ideas. Part 1 has been done for you.

PART 1   caretakers

In America, children are becoming the caretakers of their parents.

PART 2   companions

_____

PART 3   anger

_____

PART 4   mother role

_____

PART 5   nursing home

_____

6 | **LISTENING FOR DETAILS**

*Read the statements for Part 1. Then listen to Part 1 again and decide whether the statements are true or false. As you listen, write **T** or **F** next to each statement. Compare your answers with those of another student. If you disagree, listen to Part 1 again.*

PART 1

_____   1. Twenty-six-and-a-half million Americans are sixty-five years old.

_____   2. Daughters and daughters-in-law are always the caretakers of their parents.

_____   3. These caretakers go to live in their parents' homes.

Repeat the same procedure for Parts 2–5.

PART 2

_____   4. While one woman's husband went to work, she cared for her mother.

_____   5. When one woman's mother fell and broke a hip, she couldn't help her.

_____   6. Parents live longer than they used to.

_____   7. Children don't want to share the responsibilities of caring for their parents.

_____   8. Susan and her husband had already made plans for his mother to live with them before she became blind.

_____   9. Vivian had to quit a full-time job to care for her mother.

_____ 10. Vivian didn't leave the house for very long.

PART 3

_____ 11. Loving families have fewer problems caring for their aging parents.

_____ 12. Vivian's son didn't like his grandmother.

_____ 13. Susan and her husband wanted to be alone to fight.

_____ 14. Susan and Vivian joined a group to get away from their mothers.

_____ 15. Susan had conflicting feelings about caring for aging parents.

PART 4

_____ 16. Margaret didn't take care of her mother because she lived across the country in Arizona.

_____ 17. Daughters change roles with their mothers when their mothers become dependent.

_____ 18. Vivian forgot who her mother was when she introduced her.

_____ 19. Vivian was tired of her mother.

PART 5

_____ 20. Susan, Margaret, and Vivian don't like being caught in the middle of two generations.

_____ 21. The decision to put a parent in a nursing home is easier if the parent is ill.

_____ 22. Vivian's children thought a nursing home was the best solution for her mother.

_____ 23. These families couldn't handle the cost of nursing home care for their aging parents.

_____ 24. These three women want to live with their children when they can no longer care for themselves.

7   LOOKING AT LANGUAGE

■ USING *WOULD* FOR REPEATED ACTION IN THE PAST

Exercise 1

Listen to the following segment of the interview. Focus on the use of ***would*** *by these two women. Discuss the use of this verb.*

SUSAN:
> My husband ***would*** go to work, and I had my mother-in-law.

MARGARET:
> It was just taking up more and more of my time, and I was becoming just a full-time sitter for my mother. And she ***would*** fall and break a hip, or another bone, and I ***would*** have to go flying off to take care of her.

EXPLANATION

In these examples, the women are describing regularly repeated actions in the past. Notice that they use the verb ***would*** when they describe an action in their past life that was routine, habitual, or characteristic of their activities. This verb form is also used in reminiscing or telling stories about recurrent past actions.

Exercise 2

Read the following summary of the report. Past tense verbs have been italicized. Notice that some of these verbs are used to express habitual past actions. Therefore, they can be replaced by ***would*** *+ base verb. Choose the ones you think could be substituted by the* ***would*** *verb form to express recurrent actions. Circle the number under those verbs. Then compare your answers with those of another student.*

Many middle-aged women in America have become caretakers of their parents. In this interview, three women ***discussed*** their feelings about
1
becoming caretakers for their aging parents.

All three women **talked**[2] about the fact that, over the years, their aging parents **asked**[3] them to help so often that their lives **changed**[4] quite drastically. Because of this, the women's mothers eventually **moved**[5] in with their daughters and daughters-in-law and suddenly **became**[6] their constant companions. This **caused**[7] the women to feel a lot of anger because they **had**[8] to constantly reassure their aging parents. For example, Vivian's mother **used to ask**[9] her when she **expected**[10] to come home each time she **left**[11] the house. Her son, who **used to babysit**[12] his grandmother regularly, finally **said**[13] he wasn't coming home.

The women couldn't express their anger about the situation. Two of them, Susan and Vivian, **joined**[14] a support group where, each time, they **talked**[15] about their sense of duty and the guilt they **had**[16] about feeling angry and trapped. But, for medical reasons, all three women eventually **put**[17] their mothers in nursing homes.

The interviewer **described**[18] these women as "women caught in the middle of two generations" because they'd been called upon to play the role of mother once again.

Exercise 3

*Write a short essay describing a period in your childhood. Use the **would** verb form to express regularly repeated events in your life. Describe the routines you had. Think about these questions: Where would you go? Who would you go with? What would you do? When would you do it? How often would you do it?*

8 FOLLOW-UP ACTIVITIES

■ DISCUSSION QUESTIONS

In groups, discuss your answers to the following questions:

1. In facing your own old age, would you choose to live in a nursing home or with your children?

2. Susan and Vivian joined a support group to talk about their feelings with other women who were in the same situation. This is one way in which Americans deal with personal problems. What do you think about this?

■ COMPOSITION TOPICS

Choose one of the following topics:

1. Write an essay in which you describe the differences between the lifestyle and social position of aging parents in your own country and in the United States.

2. You listened to three women describe their feelings about caring for their mothers. Imagine that you are one of these aging parents. Write a letter to a friend expressing your feelings about living with your daughter. Discuss your feelings about becoming dependent.

■ CASE STUDY: HELEN

A. Taking Notes to Prepare

Listen to the report again. Take notes on the situation of the three women interviewed in the report. The women's names and some examples have been provided for you.

By focusing on the various decisions and feelings of the women in these three situations, you may be better able to understand and make suggestions in the case study that follows.

(continued on next page)

	Decisions	Feelings
Susan:	• *brought her blind mother-in-law home* • *took her everywhere; constant companion*	• *felt stress on her marriage* • *angry about losing control*
Margaret:		
Vivian:		

B. Case Study

You have listened to three American women express their feelings about caring for their aging parents. You also have your own opinions on the issue.

Work in groups. Read the following story. Then act as a group of family counselors and propose a solution to the problem. Compare your solution with those of the other groups.

HELEN

Joan and Harry live in New York. Their children are both grown up. Their daughter is away at college and their son is still living at home while he finishes his studies at the local community college.

Joan's mother, Helen, lives in California. She has lived there all her life. For the past fifteen years, she has lived alone in her own apartment. The apartment is in a special apartment complex for the aged. Helen is happy there because there are many convenient services and the people who live in the complex are very friendly.

Over the past two years, Helen's health has been quite poor. She fell twice in the last six months and had to be hospitalized. Joan, being the only child, has the responsibility of caring for her mother whenever anything goes wrong. This has meant that Joan has had to do quite a lot of transcontinental caretaking over the last two years. During Joan's last trip to California, her mother's neighbors expressed their concern about Helen's ability to care for herself. It seems that something will have to be done.

Joan has talked with her family about the possibility of bringing her mother back to New York to live with them. This would enable Helen to receive the care she needs from her daughter. However, Joan's husband, Harry, is concerned that the situation would put stress on the family. Joan's son says that he doesn't want to become a sitter for his grandmother and says he will leave home if she moves in.

Helen is afraid of flying, and she doesn't want to leave California. So Joan looked into the possibility of putting her mother in a nursing home in California. There she could receive constant care, and she would no longer have to live alone. However, the idea of putting her mother in a nursing home makes Joan feel guilty. She feels it is her duty to care for her mother. Helen, on the other hand, says she doesn't want to leave her apartment. She says she is comfortable there and doesn't want to change.

This week, Helen fell again and hurt her leg. Joan will go to California to take care of her. She will then have to decide what to do with her mother.

"Women Caught in the Middle of Two Generations" was first broadcast on "Morning Edition," October 20, 1982. The reporter is Katherine Ferguson.

THE MAIL-ORDER BRIDE

---

1 PREDICTING

From the title, discuss what you think the report is about.

2   THINK AHEAD

In groups, discuss your answers to the following questions:

1. What are the most common ways of meeting a person of the opposite sex in your country?

2. What are the responsibilities of the man and woman in a marriage?

3. Are cross-cultural marriages common in your country? Are they accepted?

3   VOCABULARY

Read the following sentences. The words in italics will help you understand the interview. Try to determine the meaning of these words from the context of the sentences. Then write a synonym or your own definition of the words.

1. In the days of the Wild West in America, both people and mail traveled by ***stagecoach*** to get from one town to the next.

_____

2. With the rising divorce rate, more and more people are becoming ***disillusioned*** with marriage. The dreamlike quality of marriage is being replaced by a harsher, less appealing reality.

_____

3. It is said that many marriages fail because the ***romance*** has gone out of the relationship. The love letters, flowers, and candlelight dinners of the early years of marriage disappear in the later years.

_____

4. After the marriage ceremony, couples will sometimes go on their ***honeymoon*** to exotic, faraway places.

_____

(continued on next page)

5. Before considering marriage, some people will look for a partner with specific *attributes*, such as good looks, wealth, or personality.

_____

6. Some men refer to women as *gals*, a term not always appreciated by women.

_____

7. To make a document legal, it is sometimes necessary to get it *notarized.*

_____

8. *Profile forms* are often used to get the personal information needed to match men and women.

_____

9. Some people who go to *singles bars* are hoping to meet someone of the opposite sex.

_____

Now try to match the words with a definition or synonym. Then compare your answers with those of another student. The first one has been done for you.

_c_ 1. stagecoach	a. personality evaluation
____ 2. disillusioned	b. vacation taken by newlyweds after marriage
____ 3. romance	
____ 4. honeymoon	c. horse-drawn vehicle
____ 5. attribute	d. disenchanted, disappointed, unhappy
____ 6. gal	
____ 7. notarized	e. recognized by law
____ 8. profile form	f. place where unmarried people meet
____ 9. singles bar	g. feeling of love
	h. woman; girl
	i. quality

4	# TASK LISTENING

Listen to the interview. Find the answer to the following question:

Where do mail-order brides come from?

5	# LISTENING FOR MAIN IDEAS

Listen to the interview again. The interview has been divided into four parts, each expressing a main idea. You will hear a beep at the end of each part. Answer the question for each part in a complete sentence. You should have four statements that make a summary of the interview. Compare your summary with that of another student.

PART 1   Why are more Asian women coming to the United States?

_____

_____

PART 2   Why do American men choose these women?

_____

_____

PART 3   How are men and women matched by Louis Florence's service?

_____

_____

PART 4   Why does Florence feel his service helps people make good marriages?

_____

_____

6   LISTENING FOR DETAILS

Read the questions for Part 1. Then listen to Part 1 again. As you listen, circle the best answer. Compare your answers with those of another student. If you disagree, listen to Part 1 again.

PART 1

1. The mail-order bride . . .

    a. traveled by stagecoach.

    b. has returned.

    c. is a new culture.

2. The number of mail-order bride services existing today is . . .

    a. 34.

    b. 3,400.

    c. Four times the original number.

3. Which is *not* true about the Florences' American-Asian Worldwide Service?

    a. It started in 1979.

    b. They have arranged nearly 715 marriages.

    c. Men can correspond with many women for about $360.

Repeat the same procedure for Parts 2–4.

PART 2

4. Why do men choose to use this service?

    a. They think marriage is an illusion.

    b. They feel American women aren't feminine enough.

    c. After four or five years of marriage with American women, they want a change.

5. Which quality does Mr. Florence attribute to Asian women?

   a. They are honorable.

   b. They are lovely.

   c. They are obedient.

6. Where would a man normally ask the questions that are on the questionnaire?

   a. in a church

   b. in a disco

   c. nowhere

7. Who wrote the personality evaluation profile?

   a. Louis Florence

   b. Tessie Florence

   c. clients who use the service

8. Which is *not* mentioned as a type of question that is asked on the questionnaire?

   a. questions concerning the woman's traditions

   b. questions concerning the woman's figure

   c. questions concerning the woman's makeup

PART 4

9. Why does Florence disagree with critics of his operation?

   a. They are in different businesses.

   b. His service offers an alternative.

   c. He offers more possibilities for meeting the opposite sex.

10. Why does Florence think his service is the best?

   a. It offers more beautiful women than does a disco or bar.

   b. It's easier than going to church.

   c. It has people correspond by letter first.

7   LOOKING AT LANGUAGE

■ IDIOMS

Exercise 1

Many idioms were used in the discussion of mail-order brides. Read the following statements as you listen to the tape. Try to determine the meaning of the italicized idioms in these sentences. Write a synonym or your own definition of each one. Then compare your answers with those of another student.

1. **INTERVIEWER:**
    Most of us think the mail-order bride ***went the way of the stagecoach***. She did, for a while. Now she's back, this time in cross-cultural form.

    _____

2. **INTERVIEWER:**
    Louis Florence says his customers are men who are disillusioned by American women.

    LOUIS FLORENCE:
    They ***are turned off***, they say, because of the lack of femininity.

    _____

3. **INTERVIEWER:**
    You've made the allusion—you seem to give the impression that you might believe that Asian women ***have a corner on*** these attributes, if that's what they are, of knowing how to please. Is that what you're saying?

LOUIS FLORENCE:

Well, from my personal experience, being married to lovely Tess, she has been brought up in the Asian culture that makes her feel as though . . . that she will love, honor, obey, and treat her husband very nicely all the time.

4. TESSIE FLORENCE:

There are some questions that most of the gentlemen ***cannot afford to*** ask the ladies. So I thought of devising those questions for our clients to submit it with their form.

5. INTERVIEWER:

You know, Mr. Florence, critics of operations, companies, businesses such as yours say you are ***peddling flesh***. How would you respond to that?

LOUIS FLORENCE:

I violently disagree. We offer an alternative to the common methods of meeting somebody of the opposite sex.

6. LOUIS FLORENCE:

Here in the United States you can go to a disco, you can go to a singles bar—which, as far as I'm concerned, are flesh markets. You can go to church, or you can sit down and go through our catalogs or run an ad and get letters from ladies. And sit there without physically and personally trying to touch her and sit and ***pour your heart out*** and write letters and get to know each other by correspondence.

7. LOUIS FLORENCE:

And our marriages, we find, are ***working out***.

Exercise 2

Now try to match the idioms with a definition or synonym.

_____ 1.	go the way of the stagecoach	a. can't put in danger
_____ 2.	be turned off	b. be disinterested
_____ 3.	have a corner on	c. sell sex
_____ 4.	cannot afford to	d. ended years ago
_____ 5.	peddle flesh	e. succeed
_____ 6.	pour your heart out	f. own
_____ 7.	work out	g. express most intimate feelings

8 FOLLOW-UP ACTIVITIES

■ DISCUSSION QUESTIONS

In groups, discuss your answers to the following questions:

1. Do you think a mail-order bride service can be a good way for people to find their mates?

2. Do you agree with Louis Florence that American women are less feminine than Asian women?

■ COMPOSITION TOPICS

Choose one of the following topics:

1. What should be considered in choosing a spouse? Write an essay in which you express your opinion.

2. Write an essay in which you describe the problems a person in your country might encounter if he or she married someone of a different culture, religion, race, or social class.

■ SIMULATION GAME: LICENSING MAIL-ORDER BRIDE SERVICES

A. Taking Notes to Prepare

Listen to the interview again. Take notes on the mail-order bride service described in the interview. Key phrases and some examples have been provided for you.

The interviewer raises some questions and concerns about this service. Louis and Tessie Florence point out its advantages. Use your notes on these two points of view to prepare the roles in the ***simulation game*** that follows.

The interviewer's point of view (questions/concerns about the service):

- *Do Asian women have a corner on knowing how to please?*

_____

_____

_____

_____

_____

The Florences' point of view (benefits offered by the service):

- *The men feel like they're on their honeymoon after four or five years.*

_____

_____

_____

_____

_____

B. Simulation Game

For this simulation game, the class is divided into two groups. One group will represent the Consumer Affairs Committee. The other group will represent the mail-order bride operators. Read the situation, choose roles, and, after a fifteen-minute preparation, begin the investigation of the mail-order bride service.

THE SITUATION

The Department of Consumer Affairs* has received complaints concerning a recently licensed mail-order bride service.

A group of people who started the service will meet with the department to decide whether or not the business should be permitted to continue operating. No doubt, the decisions made at this meeting will have a great impact on the future of mail-order bride services.

THE ROLES

DEPARTMENT OF CONSUMER AFFAIRS

You work for the Department of Consumer Affairs. You must investigate the activities of the mail-order bride service. Your recommendation could close the business.

Make a list of complaints you have received concerning the business. Prepare questions for your investigation. You may want to consider:

- Protection rights and care for the women once they are in the United States

- What happens if the man changes his mind

- What happens if the woman wants to return to her country

* *the Department of Consumer Affairs:* a government agency that protects consumers

MAIL-ORDER BRIDE SERVICE OPERATORS

You are a group of people who started a mail-order bride service this year. Your business, you believe, offers an alternative to single men who would like to meet women but who feel uncomfortable going to singles bars and discos.

Recently the Department of Consumer Affairs has contacted you concerning complaints they've received about the activities of your operation. You have not been told the exact nature of the complaints. You must meet with the department to defend the operation of your business.

Anticipate the types of complaints you think they have received. You may want to consider:

- Protection rights for the women
- Procedures taken in the case of divorce
- Support systems for the women

"The Mail-Order Bride" was first broadcast on "Morning Edition," January 29, 1984. The interviewer is Lee Thornton.

FACING THE WRONG END OF A PISTOL

9

PREDICTING

From the title, discuss what you think the interview is about.

THINK AHEAD

Work in groups. Read the following statements. Do you agree with them? See if everyone in your group has the same opinion.

1. Handguns have no other purpose than to kill people.

2. Rifles are acceptable since they are primarily used in hunting.

3. Gun manufacturers are responsible for crimes committed with guns.

4. Everyone should have the right to possess a gun for self-protection.

VOCABULARY

Exercise 1

Read the following sentences. The verbs in italics will help you understand the interview. Try to determine the meaning of these verbs from the context of the sentences. Then write a synonym or your own definition of the verbs.

1. Handguns **account for** many of the crimes that are committed in the United States.

   _____

2. Some gun manufacturers are trying to **lift the ban** against the sale of guns across state lines* because this ban has hurt their business.

   _____

3. It may be necessary to **exempt** a handgun known as the "Saturday Night Special" **from** proposals to increase gun sales, as this handgun is responsible for many crimes.

   _____

4. Some victims of gun crimes have begun **launching attacks** against the manufacturers of guns. They feel that the manufacturers are responsible for the crimes committed with guns.

   _____

* *state lines:* the borders that separate one state from another in the United States

(continued on next page)

5. Some victims of gun crimes have taken their cases to court in order to *file suit* against those whom they feel are responsible for the crime.

_____

6. Is the maker of a gun responsible for crimes committed with that gun simply because he *manufactures* it?

_____

7. Is the person who sells a gun responsible for crimes committed with that gun simply because he *distributes* it?

_____

8. If a robber wants to *hold up* a bank or store, one of the easiest weapons he can carry is a handgun.

_____

9. A robber who uses a handgun *is* usually *after* money and will only use the gun if he has to.

_____

Now try to match the verbs and verbal expressions with their definitions. Then compare your answers with those of another student. The first one has been done for you.

_i_ 1. account for   a. not include in

____ 2. lift a ban   b. take someone to court

____ 3. exempt from   c. sell

____ 4. launch an attack   d. produce; make

____ 5. file suit   e. want

____ 6. manufacture   f. rob with a weapon

____ 7. distribute   g. end a prohibition

____ 8. hold up   h. fight

____ 9. be after   i. be responsible for

Exercise 2

The following words will help you understand the crime described in the interview. Draw lines to connect the words with the part of the body they identify.

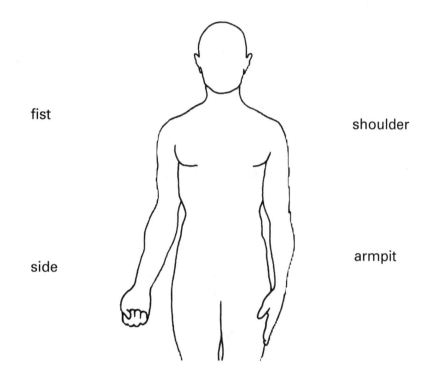

fist

shoulder

side

armpit

<table>
<tr><td>**4**</td></tr>
</table>

TASK LISTENING

Listen to the interview. Find the answer to the following question:

What is Olen Kelley's attitude toward gun control?

5 LISTENING FOR MAIN IDEAS

Listen to the interview again. The interview has been divided into three parts, each expressing a main idea. You will hear a beep at the end of each part. Answer the question for each part in a complete sentence. You should have three statements that make a summary of the interview. Compare your summary with that of another student.

PART 1   Which gun are some people trying to stop from being sold?

_____

PART 2   What happened to Kelley?

_____

PART 3   Who is Kelley suing?

_____

6 LISTENING FOR DETAILS

Read the questions for Part 1. Then listen to Part 1 again. As you listen, circle the best answer. Compare your answers with those of another student. If you disagree, listen to Part 1 again.

PART 1

1. Statistics show that many people will . . .

   a. own a handgun in their lives.

   b. be held up in their lives.

   c. commit a crime in their lives.

2. What change in the Gun Control Act is being proposed by the Senate Judiciary Committee?

   a. The sale of guns would be banned.

   b. Most bans against the sale of guns across state lines would be lifted.

   c. Only some states would sell guns.

3. Sen. Edward Kennedy tried to . . .

    a. increase the sale of Saturday Night Specials.

    b. stop the proposal from being passed.

    c. stop the sale of Saturday Night Specials.

4. Kelley . . .

    a. owns a grocery store.

    b. attacked someone.

    c. has been held up five times.

Repeat the same procedure for Parts 2 and 3.

PART 2

5. What happened when Kelley tried to open the safe the first time?

    a. He couldn't get it open.

    b. He got the money out.

    c. He took his gun.

6. What did the robbers do to Kelley?

    a. They hit him over the head with a gun.

    b. They shot him in the shoulder.

    c. They shot him in the armpit.

PART 3

7. Where is the manufacturer of the gun located?

    a. in Florida

    b. in Rome

    c. in Germany

8. What does Kelley say knives are meant to be used for?

    a. to kill people

    b. other purposes than crime

    c. sports

(continued on next page)

9. Why does Kelley criticize Saturday Night Specials?

   a. They can't be used for sports.

   b. They are hard to use.

   c. It's difficult to shoot something with them from far away.

10. Which of the following reasons does Kelley give for taking his suit to the Supreme Court*, if necessary?

   a. He has to take it to the Supreme Court.

   b. He has a lot of time.

   c. He feels he has the right to try.

11. What does Kelley hope to accomplish by taking his case to court?

   a. He wants to make $500 million.

   b. He wants to sue the lawyers.

   c. He wants to stop the manufacturer from making Saturday Night Specials.

7 LOOKING AT LANGUAGE

■ RECOGNIZING AMERICAN DIALECT

Exercise 1

There are several dialects spoken in the United States. Kelley, who comes from Maryland, speaks a southern dialect. Listen again to his description of the robbery. Fill in the blanks with the missing words. Listen as many times as necessary to complete the text. Then compare your answers with those of another student.

And I _____ the combination the first _____. So one of
          1   2
'em, with the gun, put the gun up to the side of my _____, pulled
                                                    3
the _____ back and said, "Uh, don't miss it a second time." So, I
      4

* *Supreme Court:* the highest court in the United States, with power to change the decisions made by any of the courts in the nation

slowed _____ , made sure I got the safe _____ , and then
            5   6

they told me to lay down on the _____ . Well, after
                                          7

I _____ down on the floor, they . . . one of them hit me
      8

_____ the head with something. It probably was his fist, I'm
      9

not _____ ; and the other one shot me.
         10

Exercise 2

*Practice more recognition of Kelley's dialect. Listen to him describe being
shot. As you listen, try to draw the direction in which the bullet traveled.*

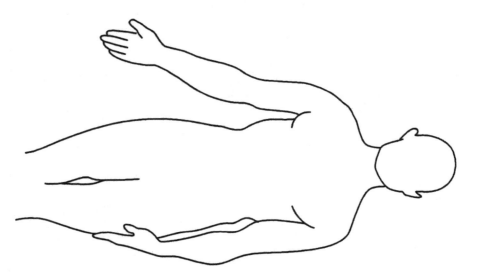

8   FOLLOW-UP ACTIVITIES

■ DISCUSSION QUESTIONS

In groups, discuss your answers to the following questions:

1. Should the sale of handguns, such as Saturday Night Specials, be
   banned?

2. Do you own a gun? Would you want to own a gun? Have you ever
   been in a situation where you wished you had a gun to protect
   yourself?

■ COMPOSITION TOPICS

Choose one of the following topics:

1. The Senate Judiciary Committee proposed changes in the 1968 Gun Control Act. These changes would allow more sales of handguns across state lines. Senator Kennedy tried to exempt Saturday Night Specials from the proposal, but he failed.

   Write a letter to Senator Kennedy, explaining why you agree or disagree with his attempt. Give reasons to support your argument.

2. The following slogan was once common on car bumper stickers:

   IF GUNS ARE OUTLAWED, ONLY OUTLAWS WILL HAVE GUNS.

   Write an essay in which you express your opinion about the slogan.

■ ROLE PLAY: THE COURTROOM

A. Taking Notes to Prepare

Listen to the interview again. Take notes on Kelley's case. Key phrases and an example have been provided for you.

Kelley has been held up several times in his grocery store, and he is now suing the gun manufacturer and the distributor. By focusing on the important details of this case and Kelley's background, you may be better able to prepare for the role play that follows.

Kelley's background:

grocery store manager in Silver Spring, Maryland

_____

_____

_____

_____

_____

The holdup:

_____

_____

_____

_____

_____

_____

_____

_____

The suit:

_____

_____

_____

_____

B. Role Play

For this role play, the class is divided into three groups. One group will prepare arguments for the defense. Another group will prepare arguments for the plaintiff. The final group will review the facts of the case and determine courtroom conduct and procedures. Read the situation, choose roles, and, after a twenty-minute preparation, begin the courtroom trial of Kelley vs. R. G. Industries.

THE SITUATION

There has been much controversy over Kelley's suit, and his case is being taken to court. The plaintiff, Kelley, is suing a manufacturer of Saturday Night Specials. He is asking $500 million in damages. The trial will begin shortly. In preparation for the trial, all the interested parties have been preparing their arguments. The result of this trial will certainly have a great impact on the future of Saturday Night Specials.

THE ROLES

GROUP A

KELLEY

Your grocery store has been held up five times. You are now suing the gun manufacturer, whom you feel is responsible for the damages. You will tell your story to the court and give reasons why you hold the gun manufacturer responsible. Try to imagine what the defense will say, in order to have a strong response.

PLAINTIFF'S ATTORNEY

You are Kelley's attorney and will represent him in his suit for $500 million. You will present arguments as to why the gun manufacturer should be held responsible. You will also prepare your client, Kelley, to respond to the accusations and questions of the defense.

EXPERT WITNESS

You are a criminal investigator. You will present data to the court indicating that an increasing number of crimes is committed with Saturday Night Specials.

GROUP B

MANUFACTURER OF SATURDAY NIGHT SPECIALS

You manufacture Saturday Night Specials. You have been accused of being responsible for damages resulting from the use of the gun you manufacture. You must present arguments to defend your case.

DEFENDANT'S ATTORNEY

You are the gun manufacturer's attorney and will represent them against the claims of the plaintiff, Kelley. You will present reasons why the gun manufacturer should not be held responsible for crimes committed with the gun. You should prepare your client, the manufacturer, to respond to the accusations and questions of the plaintiff. Try to imagine what the plaintiff will say in order to have a strong response.

EXPERT WITNESS

You are a sociologist. Present data indicating that there is no apparent correlation between crimes committed and the weapons used to commit those crimes.

GROUP C

THE JUDGES

You will listen to both sides of the issues. Try to remain objective throughout the court trial. You may reject any irrelevant or "leading" questions of the attorneys. You will quietly consult with each other to decide if the attorneys' objections are to be "overruled" or "sustained." Before the trial begins, review the facts of the case with the jurors. Decide what behavior will be permitted in the courtroom. Decide on what grounds an attorney's objections will be overruled or sustained.

Note: In the American legal system, there is one judge who rules. In this role play, two judges should be used to promote discussion in the decision-making process.

THE JURORS

You are six to twelve citizens who have been called to serve in court. You will listen to both sides of the issue, taking notes on relevant information. As a group, develop a system of note-taking to record the information given in court. You will use this information to make your decision on the case. You should disregard anything that the judge says is irrelevant. You will decide whether or not Kelley wins his suit. A majority vote is necessary for your decision.

COURTROOM PROCEDURE

1. The judge explains the case to the jury.

2. The plaintiff's attorney asks his or her expert witness to sit in the witness's chair and begins to question him or her. The defendant's attorney may then ask this witness questions. An individual attorney may question a witness for no more than three minutes. It is suggested that each attorney be timed.

3. The defendant's attorney asks his or her expert witness to sit in the witness's chair and begins to question him or her. The plaintiff's attorney may then ask this witness questions.

4. The plaintiff's attorney questions the plaintiff (Kelley). The defendant's attorney may then ask him questions.

5. The defendant's attorney questions the defendant (the gun manufacturer). The plaintiff's attorney may then ask him or her questions.

6. The defendant's attorney sums up his or her side of the case.

7. The plaintiff's attorney sums up his or her side of the case.

8. The jury deliberates in private. Jury members compare notes and argue over the details of the case. They then vote for or against the plaintiff. A majority vote rules.

9. The jury presents its decision to the court.

USEFUL WORDS AND EXPRESSIONS

When people speak to the judge, they say:

- Your honor.

When an attorney speaks to the judge, the attorney may say:

- I object! (The attorney is telling the judge that he/she feels the other attorney is asking questions that are not relevant to the case.)

- The plaintiff/defense rests its case. (The attorney is telling the judge that there are no more witnesses to be questioned.)

When a judge speaks to an attorney, the judge may say:

- Call your next witness. (The judge is asking the attorney to question a new witness.)

- Overruled! (The judge is telling the attorney that he/she does not agree with the attorney's objection, and therefore the other attorney may continue asking those questions.)

- Sustained! (The judge is telling the attorney that he/she agrees with the attorney's objection, and therefore the other attorney may not continue asking those questions.)

When a witness speaks to the attorney, the witness may say:

- I plead the Fifth.* (The witness is telling the attorney that he or she doesn't want to answer the attorney's questions. This is a legal right of the witness.)

---

* *The Fifth:* The Fifth Amendment to the U.S. Constitution excuses people from testifying against themselves in court proceedings.

"Facing the Wrong End of a Pistol" was first broadcast on "All Things Considered," April 24, 1982. The interviewer is Leslie Breeding.

WHAT CONSTITUTES A FAMILY?

1

PREDICTING

From the title, discuss what you think the interview is about.

2   THINK AHEAD

Work in groups. Read the following statements. Do you agree with them? See if everyone in your group has the same opinion.

1. The traditional family, in which the father works and the wife stays home to care for the children, is the ideal family.

2. Gay, or same-sex, couples should be legally recognized as a family.

3. Nontraditional families will eventually be more common than the traditional nuclear family, that is, a family made up of parents and children.

3   VOCABULARY

The following words will help you understand the interview. Try to guess the meaning of these words from your knowledge of English, or use your dictionary. In each set of words, cross out the word that does not have a similar meaning. Then compare your answers with those of another student. Discuss the relationship between the words in each set. The first one has been done for you.

1. **wage-earning**	~~volunteer-working~~	money-making	income-producing
2. **species**	type	group	member
3. **foster parents**	biological parents	caretakers	adoptive parents
4. **stepfamily**	alternative family	nuclear family	nontraditional family
5. **profile**	description	picture	light
6. **raise**	bring up	rise	educate
7. **seniors**	aged	elderly	middle-aged
8. **championed**	supported	defended	fought against

(continued on next page)

9. **grapple with**	ignore	confront	face
10. **evict**	expel	reject	invite
11. **legitimize**	legalize	cancel	justify
12. **dependent**	guardian	child	descendant

4 | TASK LISTENING

Listen to the interview. Find the answer to the following question:

> Give two examples of nontraditional families mentioned in the report.

5 | LISTENING FOR MAIN IDEAS

Listen to the interview again. The interview has been divided into four parts, each expressing a main idea. You will hear a beep at the end of each part. Answer the question for each part in a complete sentence. You should have four statements that make a summary of the report. Compare your summary with that of another student.

PART 1   What legal action has been taken in California?

_____

PART 2   How does Shannon Gibson's family situation illustrate the situation of many American families today?

_____

PART 3   What issue will the courts be grappling with for years to come?

_____

PART 4   How does the family registration certificate help legal guardians such as John Brown?

_____

6 | LISTENING FOR DETAILS

Read the questions for Part 1. Then listen to Part 1 again. As you listen, circle the best answer. Compare your answers with those of another student. If you disagree, listen to Part 1 again.

PART 1

1. What is disappearing in the United States?

   a. a family with a working father and a mother who stays home to raise children

   b. the percentage of kids born to each family

   c. institutions that recognize alternative families

2. Which nontraditional groups are mentioned as people living together as families?

   a. same-sex partners

   b. friends sharing housing

   c. families with adopted children

Repeat the same procedure for Parts 2–4.

PART 2

3. How is Shannon Gibson like many other sixth graders?

   a. She chews gum.

   b. She has a stepmother.

   c. She visits her father twice a month.

4. What concern does Shannon have?

   a. that her mother will soon die

   b. that she will have to live with her biological father again

   c. that she wouldn't be able to see her stepfather someday

(continued on next page)

5. How can a group register as a family in California?

   a. They must meet with the secretary of state.

   b. They must pay a $100 fee.

   c. They must fill out a form.

6. Which group is ***not*** mentioned as one that can register with California's secretary of state as a family?

   a. stepfamilies

   b. heterosexual couples

   c. unrelated seniors

PART 3

7. What did The Family Diversity Project champion?

   a. the idea of private agencies defending the rights of the family

   b. the concept of nontraditional family registration

   c. the old concept of a family

8. What event caused the state of New York to reconsider the definition of *family*?

   a. a housing survivor case* in which a person was to be evicted

   b. the disappearance of rent-controlled apartments

   c. a court case involving an adoption

9. Which group is ***not*** mentioned as a group in California that can register its name as an association?

   a. a labor union

   b. an herb society

   c. a family

* a case that determines whether or not a person living in an apartment or house may remain living in that apartment or house (and pay the same rent) after the legal tenant has died

10. Which two states have registration procedures similar to those in California?

    a. Oregon and Washington

    b. New York and New Jersey

    c. Virginia and West Virginia

PART 4

11. How significant is the certificate itself?

    a. It has important legal benefits.

    b. It has no legal benefits.

    c. It has legal benefits for fathers.

12. What role does John Brown play as a parent?

    a. He is an adoptive father.

    b. He and his wife are legal guardians.

    c. He has four dependents.

13. What concern does Brown have about his parenting role?

    a. He is afraid his son won't be able to go to college.

    b. He wants to continue to claim his college-aged son as a dependent on his insurance policy.

    c. He is afraid he will lose his status as guardian for his college-aged son.

14. What is likely to happen to Brown as a result of his certificate?

    a. The Internal Revenue Service will not consider his son as a dependent.

    b. His insurance company will refuse to sell him insurance.

    c. His nontraditional family will be accepted.

| 7 | **LOOKING AT LANGUAGE** |

■ PRESENT UNREAL CONDITIONAL

Exercise 1

Listen to the following segment of the interview. Focus on the use of ***would*** *in Shannon Gibson's statements. What situation is she reacting to? What condition(s) are implied in her statements?*

SHANNON:

   Pat is not my biological father, but he's raised me since I was two years old. So, it ***wouldn't be*** right . . . that I ***wouldn't be able*** to see him or anything like that.

EXPLANATION

In the statements ***it wouldn't be right*** and ***I wouldn't be able to see him***, she is reacting to an unreal situation, a situation that she imagines could happen. Although she does not say this, the following conditions are implied:

   If my mother died, . . .

   If my stepfather didn't get visitation rights, . . .

The present unreal conditional is usually formed as follows:

Condition Clause	*Result Clause*
If + subject + past tense	subject + ***would*** + base verb
If my mother died, . . .	it wouldn't be right. . . .
If my stepfather didn't get visitation rights, . . .	I wouldn't be able to see him.

Exercise 2

Complete the sentences, expressing your opinion about traditional and nontraditional families. Use the present unreal pattern in each sentence.

1. If someone made a profile of traditional families in my

   country, _____

   _____ .

2. If gay couples or unrelated seniors wanted to be recognized officially

   as families in my country, _____

   _____ .

3. If California's policy of registering nontraditional families were

   instituted in my country, _____

   _____ .

4. If I were asked what constitutes a family, _____

   _____ .

5. If the nuclear family disappeared, _____

   _____ .

8 # FOLLOW-UP ACTIVITIES

▣ DISCUSSION QUESTIONS

In groups, discuss your answers to the following questions:

1. Why, in your opinion, is the traditional family disappearing in the United States?

2. What is your reaction to California's public registration of nontraditional families?

3. Would you become a member of a nontraditional family? If so, under what circumstances?

■ COMPOSITION TOPICS

Choose one of the following topics:

1. Write an essay in which you compare and contrast family life in your own country with your impressions of family life in America.

2. In the early 1970s, David Cooper wrote a book entitled *The Death of the Family*, in which he discussed alternatives to the traditional family. In his critique of the nuclear family, he makes the statement, "We don't need mother and father anymore. We only need mothering and fathering."

   Do you agree or disagree with this statement? Write an essay in which you express your opinion.

3. Should the government have the right to determine what constitutes a family? Write an essay in which you express your opinion.

■ CONDUCT A SURVEY: WHAT CONSTITUTES A FAMILY?

A. Taking Notes to Prepare

Listen to the interview again. Take notes on California's new registration policy for nontraditional families. Key phrases and some examples have been provided for you.

Although California has officially recognized nontraditional groups as families, not everyone would agree with California's definition of family, that is, any group of people living together. By taking notes on the specific groups mentioned in the interview and on their reasons for registering as "families," you may be better able to formulate questions and interpret public opinion in the survey that follows.

Examples of nontraditional families:

- *gay couples*
  _____

_____

_____

_____

_____

_____

Reasons nontraditional families want to register as a family:

    • *visitation rights*

_____

_____

_____

B. Survey

Work in groups. Write a questionnaire. Formulate five yes/no questions that will ask people's opinions about what constitutes a family. Your group will interview a cross section of people. Decide where and when you will conduct the survey, how many people you will question, who they will be, etc.

*For your survey, you will want to tally the **yes** and **no** responses as well as note any significant comments that people make. The following grid can be used to write your questions, tally responses, and record comments. An example has been provided.*

Questions	Yes	No	Comments
Do you think gay couples qualify as a family?	*///*	*//*	*They have the same rights as heterosexual couples.*

ORAL REPORT

*When your group meets again, summarize the information you've
gathered from each question. Prepare an oral report to present to the rest
of the class. Be sure to include an introduction to your survey, a
summary of the results you've gathered, and a conclusion including your
own interpretation of your findings.*

ORAL PRESENTATION PROCEDURES

1. The first student introduces the group and gives an introduction to the
   survey that was conducted.

2. The next few students present one or two of the questions that were
   asked, statistics or general responses that were received, and
   interesting comments that were made by the people who were
   interviewed. The comments mentioned should help explain why
   people answered the way they did.

3. The last student concludes the presentation by summarizing the
   findings from the survey, interpreting them, and perhaps reacting to
   the results. (For example, "We were surprised to learn that most
   people thought . . .")

USEFUL WORDS AND PHRASES

When you talk about the people who answered your survey, you can call
them:

- interviewees
- respondents

When you report the information you gathered, you can begin:

- They agreed that . . .
- They felt that . . .
- They believed that . . .
- They stated that . . .

When you indicate the number of people surveyed, you can say:

- More than half agreed that . . .
- Over 50 percent of the sample stated that . . .
- Less than a third said that . . .

**"What Constitutes a Family?" was first broadcast on "Weekend All Things
Considered," December 15, 1990. The reporter is Kitty Felde.**

FINDING DISCRIMINATION WHERE ONE WOULD HOPE TO FIND RELIEF

11

PREDICTING

From the title, discuss what you think the interview is about.

THINK AHEAD

*Work in groups. Read the following statements. Do you **agree** or **disagree** with them? See if everyone in your group has the same opinion.*

1. If a person knowingly exposes another person to the virus that causes AIDS, he or she should be punished by law.

2. Insurance companies should be required to sell insurance to all clients at the same cost, regardless of whether they have AIDS or the virus that causes the disease.

3. Discrimination against AIDS victims is as serious as discrimination against people of different races.

VOCABULARY

Read the text. The words in italics will help you understand the interview that follows. Try to determine the meaning of these words. Then match the words with their definitions or synonyms in the list at the end of the text. Write the number of each word next to its definition or synonym. The first one has been done for you.

AIDS victims suffer knowing that there is not yet a cure for their disease; it is **terminal.** To add to this suffering, AIDS victims often experience discrimination: They might not be hired for a job or they may lose a job if it is known that they have AIDS; they may not be able to rent apartments as easily as they could without the disease; the courts will often **convict** people who have purposely spread the AIDS virus, imposing unusually **harsh sentences** on them; and insurance companies may refuse to offer health or life insurance **coverage** to clients who indicate that they are **HIV positive** and, therefore, at high risk of getting AIDS.

Although many concerns about spreading the AIDS virus are ***legitimate*** (it is expected that by the end of this century, 40 million

6
people will have the disease), discrimination towards AIDS victims is often based on ***myths*** about how the virus is spread. Decisions not to

7
protect AIDS victims often come from ***prejudiced*** beliefs about who gets

8
the disease and how easily it is ***transmitted*** from person to person. Even

9
more disturbing is that this ***repugnant*** discrimination expressed towards

10
AIDS victims is often ***veiled*** with excuses of an employer's or company's

11
inability to pay for or deal with AIDS cases. For example, employees who are ***entitled*** to a job with health benefits are sometimes denied these

12
benefits when their employer discovers they have AIDS.

In the courts, there are some cases where AIDS victims have ***inflicted*** the disease ***on*** another person (by biting the person's skin or by

13
splattering the person with their blood). Even though everyone would

14
agree that these are horrible acts, the courts have often imposed unreasonable penalties on these criminals. By focusing on the AIDS victim's ***intent*** to spread his or her disease, they define the spread of the

15
disease as a criminal act.

_____ intention

_____ having the virus that may develop into AIDS

_____ stories not based on facts

_*1*_ causing death; fatal

_____ opinionated without sufficient knowledge

_____ given something unwanted to someone; imposed something on someone

(continued on next page)

_____ severe punishments given in a court of law to convicted criminals

_____ reasonable; justifiable in the eyes of the law

_____ causing ill-feeling because of real or apparent injustice; disgusting

_____ passed on

_____ hidden behind

_____ declare somebody is guilty in a court of law

_____ throwing around something liquid

_____ financial protection

_____ given a right to

4   TASK LISTENING

Listen to the interview. Find the answer to the following question:

> Is Larry Gosten sympathetic or unsympathetic toward AIDS victims who commit crimes?

5   LISTENING FOR MAIN IDEAS

Listen to the interview again. The interview has been divided into five parts, each expressing a main idea. You will hear a beep at the end of each part. Answer the question for each part in a complete sentence. You should have five statements that make a summary of the report. Compare your summary with that of another student.

PART 1   Where can we find discrimination against AIDs victims?

_____

PART 2   According to Gosten, what is the court's atitude toward AIDS victims who commit crimes?

_____

PART 3   How have AIDS victims been treated by insurance companies and employers?

_____

PART 4   Other than fear, where does much of this discrimination come from?

_____

PART 5   How does Gosten see AIDS discrimination?

_____

6 ## LISTENING FOR DETAILS

Read the questions for Part 1. Then listen to Part 1 again. As you listen, circle the best answer. Compare your answers with those of another student. If you disagree, listen to Part 1 again.

PART 1

1. What additional problem do AIDS victims suffer along with the disease?

    a. health problems with another virus

    b. discrimination

    c. rejection from their families

2. Who or what has shown that discrimination against AIDS victims exists?

    a. a study conducted by the National AIDS Program Office

    b. judges

    c. accused AIDS victims

Repeat the same procedure for Parts 2–5 on pages 120–121.

PART 2

3. How many cases has Gosten seen in which HIV was transmitted from the criminal to the victim?

   a. 200

   b. over 200

   c. zero

4. According to Gosten, why are we convicting persons with AIDS?

   a. because their behavior is irrational

   b. because we are afraid their disease will be transmitted to others

   c. because we know they will die anyway

5. What is the issue that the courts focus on?

   a. the criminal's intent to inflict AIDS on someone else

   b. the impossibility of transmission

   c. the discrimination toward these criminals

6. How does Gosten explain the behavior of the man with AIDS who tried to spread the virus?

   a. He was unconscious.

   b. He wanted to die in prison.

   c. He was desperate.

PART 3

7. Which of the following is true?

   a. There are lots of new treatments for AIDS.

   b. The public is ignorant about AIDS treatment.

   c. People can now afford new treatments for the disease.

8. What did the employer do in the case discussed by Gosten?

   a. They fired an employee with AIDS.

   b. They refused to cover an employee with AIDS.

   c. They took away some of the insurance coverage for an employee with AIDS.

PART 4

9. Which of the following is *not* mentioned about people's fear of AIDS?

   a. It springs from a deep place.

   b. They know that there isn't a zero risk.

   c. They can't be sure of tests for AIDS.

10. How does discrimination stem from economics?

   a. Food for AIDS patients is too expensive.

   b. Employers feel they must pay for too much insurance.

   c. AIDS patients can't afford the clinics.

PART 5

11. What used to be legitimate in the United States?

   a. racial separation in restaurants

   b. racial separation in courts

   c. racial discrimination in society

12. What point does Gosten make about a society that lives with AIDS?

   a. We can't do the right thing.

   b. All people should be allowed to hold a job.

   c. Some people might have to be excluded from certain everyday activities.

7 | LOOKING AT LANGUAGE

■ VERBS + PREPOSITION

Exercise

Many common expressions are made up of a verb followed by a preposition. In this interview, several examples of verb + preposition were used. Complete these sentences with a preposition from the list below. Some prepositions can be used more than once. Each sentence expresses an idea presented in the interview.

about	by	from	to
against	for	on	

1. In addition to the health problems brought on _____ AIDS, people with the HIV virus must face discrimination.

2. Many people who have tested positive _____ the HIV virus will ultimately get AIDS.

3. The courts often focus _____ the issue of "intent."

4. When a person's intent is to inflict the HIV virus _____ another person, the courts hand down unusually harsh penalties.

5. You can't really punish somebody _____ something that's impossible.

6. The person who tried to commit suicide was really crying out _____ help.

7. Discrimination springs _____ a very deep place inside people.

8. Discrimination stems _____ economics as well as fear.

9. Health-care and restaurant employers say they are not prejudiced _____ employees with AIDS but that they don't have the expertise to handle them.

10. Restaurant owners used to discriminate _____ African Americans by not serving them.

11. All people are entitled _____ a job if they can work.

12. AIDS victims should not be excluded _____ everyday life.

13. To *not* allow AIDS victims to continue work is to sentence them _____ something even worse than their terminal illness.

14. Larry Gosten is concerned _____ the discrimination the courts and insurance companies express toward AIDS victims.

8 FOLLOW-UP ACTIVITIES

▓ DISCUSSION QUESTIONS

In groups, discuss your answers to the following questions.

1. Gosten's final comment in the interview is:

   That's sentencing them to something even worse than the terminal illness they have.

   Do you agree that suffering from discrimination can be worse than suffering from a fatal disease?

2. Do you agree that an employer's refusal to hire an employee with AIDS or who is HIV positive is a "veiled form of discrimination?"

▓ COMPOSITION TOPICS

Choose one of the following topics:

1. Write an essay in which you describe the effect that AIDS has had on people living in your country.

2. How are issues of discrimination similar or different? Compare and contrast cases of discrimination (racial, sex, age, AIDS) with which you are familiar.

■ CASE STUDY: MICHAEL EVANS

A. Taking Notes to Prepare

Listen to the interview again. Take notes on Gosten's study. Key phrases and some examples have been provided for you.

The study shows that AIDS discrimination exists in precisely those places where AIDS victims would expect to find some relief. By focusing on the degree of discrimination AIDS victims face, you may be better able to evaluate the case study that follows.

The courts:

> • *reinforce myths about how AIDS is transmitted*
>
> • *judges rule spitting & biting as serious crimes when accused has AIDS*

Insurance companies:

Employers:

_____

_____

_____

Society:

_____

_____

_____

_____

B. Case Study

You have listened to Gosten's concerns about discrimination in courts, by employers, and by insurance companies.

Work in groups. Read the following story. Then act as members of an AIDS support group. Decide what advice you would give Michael Evans: Should he continue to keep his secret or not? Compare your opinion with those of the other groups.

MICHAEL EVANS

Michael Evans is a forty-year-old doctor. He has a secret: He is HIV positive. He has not yet told his patients of his illness. If anyone found out that he had AIDS, his reputation would probably be severely hurt and his career would be finished. If Evans lost his job, he could face the last years of his life not only fighting a fatal illness, but also living without a salary or health insurance. Yet,

---

(continued on next page)

MICHAEL EVANS (*continued from page 125*)

if he continues to keep his illness a secret, it might eventually be discovered and his practice could be destroyed through lawsuits.

Evans has a reason for keeping his secret. He knows that if his patients have a choice between seeing an infected doctor and seeing a healthy doctor, they will most likely choose the latter. What's more, there have been several cases in which doctors have been sued by their patients, once they announced that they had AIDS. Moreover, once an insurance company finds out that a doctor has AIDS, his or her malpractice insurance can be canceled. A recent study showed that 67 percent of HIV-positive doctors said they even avoided seeking treatment for their disease because of fear of public reaction.

Health care workers have become suspect ever since a twenty-two-year-old woman, Kimberly Bergalis, caught the HIV virus, probably from her dentist when she had a tooth removed. Since her death, as well as the deaths of other patients, many people have viewed doctors with AIDS as criminals. Many people believe that health care workers should no longer practice their profession when they know that they have AIDS. Patients feel they have the right to know if their doctor is infected with the AIDS virus, and the right to protect themselves from any danger of getting the disease.

So far, research has shown that HIV-infected health workers are not a significant threat to patients. Unless their blood is directly transferred to their patients, there is no danger of transmission of the disease. Yet, the public continues to be fearful of the possibility.

A recent proposal was made to enforce criminal penalties on any doctors or health care workers with AIDS who have not informed their patients of their disease. If Evans continues to keep his disease a secret, he might one day go to prison.

What is most difficult for Evans is the fact that he went into the medical profession with the hope of helping people, but now he must consider the fact that he could give them a terminal disease. He continues to live with his secret, taking care of his patients as usual. He takes his own medication and talks on the phone with his own doctor when no one is around in his office. Some patients have asked him why he has started wearing gloves when he takes their blood. He explains that he is not afraid of AIDS but that wearing gloves makes everybody feel more comfortable in our present world of the AIDS epidemic.

"Finding Discrimination Where One Would Hope to Find Relief" was first broadcast on "All Things Considered," January 19, 1992. The interviewer is Lynn Neary.

GREEN CONSUMERISM

The National #1 Bestseller!

50 SIMPLE THINGS YOU CAN DO TO SAVE THE EARTH

THE EARTH·WORKS GROUP

---

1 | **PREDICTING**

From the title, discuss what you think the interview is about.

2 | **THINK AHEAD**

In groups, discuss your answers to the following questions:

1. Have you made any changes in your daily life that reflect a concern for the environment? If so, what are they?

2. How much of an impact has the environmental movement had on your country? How does it compare with what's happening in other countries?

3. Have you seen any examples of false advertising for protecting the environment? If so, give examples.

3 | **VOCABULARY**

Read the text. The words in italics will help you understand the interview. Try to determine the meaning of these words. Then match the words with their definitions or synonyms in the list at the end of the text. Write the number of each word next to its definition or synonym. The first one has been done for you.

In recent decades we have become more aware of all the problems that

humans have created for the earth. Ozone depletion, acid rain, the

greenhouse effect, and deforestation are only some of the environmental

issues that were unknown three decades ago.

With all these environmental problems, people have begun to look

for ways to save the earth. ***Consciousness-raising*** groups have been
                                              ₁
formed, whose work is primarily to get each and every one of us to realize

that we have a part to play in helping to save the planet. Even small

changes in the way we live can help to save the earth. For example, many

(continued on next page)

families now turn food waste into ***compost*** rather than throw it away as
garbage. Compost can then be put back into the soil to help gardens
grow.

Yet environmental ***watchdogs*** tell us that we must be careful not to
jump too quickly ***on the*** green ***bandwagon***. One ***pitfall*** to contributing
in small ways to help save the environment is that we may feel a false
sense of ***complacency.*** How many of us end up feeling good and
satisfied that we have helped save the earth after only recycling our cans
and bottles, for example? The real tasks in saving the planet are much
greater than just recycling.

Another problem environmentalists point out is that just because a
product claims that it is "environmentally safe" does not mean that using
it is really good for the environment. They point out that, even in the area
of environmental protection, there are dishonest people trying to make
their own profit out of a good cause: ***Hucksters*** exist in all areas of life.
We must be ***leery*** of "***greenwash***" and those people who falsely advertise
or claim environmental concern where it doesn't exist. In the area of
green consumerism, this is especially important. For example, Texaco has
offered its customers a free tree ***seedling*** for the purchase of gas. The
message here is that if you plant a tree you will help make the earth a
greener place. But the gas we buy from Texaco will continue to harm the
earth.

We need to convince corporations to change their policies,
revitalize our transportation systems, and generally just consume less of
everything if we're really going to make a difference.

_____ young plant newly grown

_____ bring back to life

_____ natural fertilizer

_____ persons interested in making their own profit

_1_ making people aware of issues

_____ unethical advertising for the environment

_____ join what seems to be successful

_____ danger

_____ self-satisfaction

_____ people who look for illegal or wasteful practices or dishonest behavior

_____ suspicious; wary

---

4   TASK LISTENING

Listen to the interview. You will hear some examples of absurd advertising. As you listen, draw lines to connect each product with its false advertising promise.

Product	False Advertising Promise
gasoline	eat good cereal
cars	save the environment
candy	encourage new values

---

5   LISTENING FOR MAIN IDEAS

Listen to the interview again. The interview has been divided into five parts, each expressing a main idea. You will hear a beep at the end of each part. A word or phrase has been given for each part to help you focus on the main idea. Write the main idea in your own words. You should have five statements that make a summary of the report. Compare your summary with that of another student. Part 1 has been done for you.

(continued on next page)

PART 1   false complacency

Consumers may feel a false sense of

complacency by only shopping differently.

PART 2   shopping

_____

PART 3   longer-term issue

_____

PART 4   green marketing

_____

PART 5   revitalizing

_____

6   LISTENING FOR DETAILS

Read the statements for Part 1. Then listen to Part 1 again. As you listen, circle the best answer. Compare your answers with those of another student. If you disagree, listen to Part 1 again.

PART 1

1. Which of these book titles is *not* mentioned in the introduction to the interview?

   a. *The Green Consumer*

   b. *Shopping for a Better World*

   c. *Fifteen Simple Things You Can Do to Save the Planet*

2. What general purpose do these books have?

   a. to broaden the environmental movement

   b. to make our ordinary lives more complete

   c. to lull consumers into a false complacency

3. What do Alan Durning and Alice Tepper Marlin have in common?

   a. They are both researchers at the World Watch Institute.

   b. They are both members of the Council on Economic Priorities.

   c. They are both authors of the book *Shopping for a Better World.*

Repeat the same procedure for Parts 2–5.

PART 2

4. What one thing does Tepper Marlin feel we can do to help the environment?

   a. consume less

   b. grow better foods

   c. throw away the compost heap

5. What should we do when we shop?

   a. not use shopping carts

   b. change the places where we shop

   c. look at product contents

PART 3

6. How does Alan Durning *truly* feel about the advice on shopping?

   a. It's a really great idea.

   b. It's only a first step.

   c. It's a good long-term goal.

7. Who is responsible for overconsumption, according to Durning?

   a. one hundred billion people in developing countries

   b. people living in developed countries

   c. the majority of the world's population

(continued on next page)

8. Which of the earth's environmental problems is *not* mentioned?

a. greenhouse effect

b. acid rain

c. deforestation

9. What specific solution does Durning propose?

a. We need to consume our way out of this.

b. We have to shift our emphasis to gross consumption.

c. We have to simplify our lifestyles.

PART 4

10. How does Durning see green consuming?

a. He thinks it's like rearranging the deck chairs on the *Titanic.**

b. He thinks it's an initial educational step.

c. He is critical of it.

11. Where do we see a lot of "greenwash" going on?

a. in corporate advertising

b. at tree farms

c. in supermarkets

12. Which of the following areas is *not* mentioned as an area where we can find hucksters?

a. in health clubs

b. in food marketing

c. in green consumerism

* *Titanic:* a passenger ship that sank and in which many people died. The message in this statement is that simply changing the position of the chairs would not have saved the ship; it would have required much more. Likewise, green consuming will not be enough to save the earth.

13. How does Tepper Marlin suggest we deal with hucksters?

   a. We need to throw out the entire concept of green consumerism.

   b. Consumers need to listen to hucksters.

   c. Federal guidelines need to be established.

PART 5

14. What negative result could occur from the green-consuming movement?

   a. People won't feel good.

   b. Yuppies* will stop recycling bottles and newspapers.

   c. People won't do as much as they need to do.

15. What example does Toyota use for green advertising?

   a. Their cars have a new series of valves.

   b. Their cars don't need excess gas.

   c. People who drive their cars have the right values.

16. What does Durning think we need to focus on?

   a. reforming transportation

   b. limiting public transportation

   c. controlling rail transportation

17. What happened in the 1980s, according to Durning?

   a. We didn't reach the people who wanted to help.

   b. We focused too much on little things.

   c. We began to make a difference.

---

* Young urban professionals; *yuppies* has also taken on a negative sense in referring to young people who focus a great deal on material wealth.

7   LOOKING AT LANGUAGE

■ CAUSATIVE VERB FORM

Exercise 1

Listen to the following statements made in the interview:

1. It seems to me that the green-consuming movement could get people just sort of feeling good about what they're doing. . . .

   This sentence could be rewritten:

   It seems to me that the green-consuming movement could ***get*** people ***to feel*** good about what they're doing. . . .

2. There's a definite risk that this will ***make*** us ***feel*** better than we really are. But it's a risk that we have to take.

How do the two verb forms in italics differ in terms of meaning and form?

EXPLANATION

When something or someone causes others to do something, we use ***make***, ***have***, or ***get***.

In the two examples above, there is a small difference in meaning between "***get*** people to feel" and "***make*** us feel." ***Get*** expresses persuasion. ***Make*** expresses force or pressure; it has a stronger meaning.

In addition, ***have*** can be used in situations of authority. It is often used when one person employs another for service:

The public should ***have*** the government pass regulations to protect the environment.

Notice how active sentences are formed with these causative verbs:

base form
have or ***make*** + someone + **do** + something (example: ***have*** or ***make*** the government **pass** laws)

infinitive form
get + someone + **to do** + something (example: ***get*** the senators **to pass** laws)

Notice how passive sentences are formed with these causative verbs:

past participle

have or *get* + something + **done** (example: *have* or *get* regulations **passed**)

Exercise 2

*To save the earth, there are many things we can do at home, school, or work. Use the following cues to form complete sentences with **have**, **make**, or **get**, and make suggestions for saving the earth. Use active sentences in 1–6 and passive sentences in 7–10 to express your own ideas about how we can influence others to help save the earth. The first one has been done for you.*

1. our family/consume

    We can get our families to consume less energy at home.

2. the government/pass laws

3. our community/change

4. our friends/take important steps

5. our supermarkets/sell

6. our politicians/consider

7. trees/plant

8. transportation systems/revitalize

(continued on next page)

9. products/label

_____

10. advertising/control

_____

8 | FOLLOW-UP ACTIVITIES

◼ DISCUSSION QUESTIONS

In groups, discuss your answers to the following questions:

1. Do you believe that green consuming is a "vehicle for raising people's consciousness?" Why or why not?

2. Alan Durning states that "we at the top are the problem." Do you agree that industrialized countries have more of a responsibility toward saving the earth than developing countries do? Why or why not?

◼ COMPOSITION TOPICS

Choose one of the following topics:

1. Write a letter to either Texaco or Toyota expressing your view on their green advertising.

2. To what extent should individuals contribute to saving the earth? How much should we each change our lifestyles to improve the environment? Write an essay in which you express your opinion.

◼ VALUES CLARIFICATION: TO SAVE THE EARTH

A. Taking Notes to Prepare

Listen to the interview again. Take notes on the practical suggestions that are given for protecting the environment. Key areas of concern have been listed for you. Write the suggestions that relate to each concern. In the right-hand column, indicate whether the interviewees express a positive (+) or negative (−) view of the suggestion.

By focusing on these suggestions and whether they are seen as important for saving the environment, you may be better able to clarify your values in the exercise that follows.

	Practical Suggestions for Saving the Environment	**+ or –**
Consumption:	• *we should consume less*	+
Planting the earth:		
Education and public policy:		
Recycling:		
Transportation:		

B. Values Clarification

A few years ago, a book was published to help people get involved in protecting the environment. *50 Simple Things You Can Do to Save the Earth* quickly became a national bestseller. Other publications included *100 Ways You Can Save the World* and *101 Ways to Heal the Earth*. Below you will find thirty simple things you can do.

Work in groups. Read the list of things you can do to save the earth. Then categorize them into five general areas of concern: consumption, planting the earth, education and public policy, recycling, and transportation.

After you have categorized the items into the five general areas, rank each of the general areas in the order of most important (1) to least important ways to "save the earth." Try to reach a group consensus. Present your categories and ranking to the rest of the class.

1. Buy plain white toilet paper, tissues, and paper towels. Dyed paper pollutes.

2. Walk or ride a bike instead of using the car for short trips.

3. Keep your car tires inflated to the proper pressure to improve fuel economy.

4. Turn off lights in rooms you aren't using.

5. Plant trees. This can reduce heating and cooling bills, help prevent soil erosion, and reduce air pollution.

6. Investigate the environmental record of companies you invest in. Write a letter as a shareholder to the company president, or sell your stock.

7. Return your recyclable cans and bottles for your deposit.

8. Share rides to work, or use public transportation.

9. Buy a fuel-efficient car: thirty-five miles per gallon.

10. Read labels and research the products you buy.

11. Buy products packaged in recycled paper or cardboard.

12. Limit your use of "disposable" items.

13. Close off unused areas of your home. Shut off or block heat vents.

14. Compare energy-guide labels when buying appliances.

15. Tune up your car regularly for maximum gas mileage.

16. Learn about global climate change.

17. Rent or borrow items you don't often use. Efficient use of products conserves resources.

18. Avoid products made from tropical-rainforest woods.

19. Instead of toxic mothballs, buy cedar chips.

20. Don't litter. Pick up any garbage you see, especially plastic rings that can trap birds and fish.

21. Join an environmental organization.

22. Buy recycled paper products, stationery, and greeting cards.

23. Shop at your local farmers' market. Products are fresh, packaging is minimal, and foods are less likely to be contaminated with preservatives and pesticides.

24. Start an organic garden.

25. Buy in bulk to avoid overpackaging.

26. Avoid optional equipment on cars that decreases fuel economy.

27. Urge your community to start a recycling program.

28. Start a recycling program where you work.

29. Give leftover paint to theater groups, schools, or church groups.

30. Educate your children about the environment.

Excerpted from *Iowa Energy Bulletin*'s list of "100 Ways You Can Save the Earth"

"Green Consumerism" was first broadcast on "Living on Earth," May 3, 1991. The interviewer is Steve Curwood.

TAPESCRIPT

UNIT 1
GIVE ME MY PLACE TO SMOKE!

Michael: My name is Michael, and I've been smoking for fifteen years.

Peggy: My name's Peggy, and I've been smoking for probably thirty to thirty-five years.

Katie Davis: Peggy and Michael sit in a smoky neighborhood bar in Washington, D.C., a cigarette perched in each of their hands. They say there are fewer and fewer places like this, where they feel completely comfortable lighting up, and they expect the EPA report on second-hand smoke to contribute to further restrictions on smoking in public places. They both say they are keenly aware of the reception they get when they smoke, and how that has changed over the years.

Peggy: Thirty-five years ago you really didn't give a lot of thought to smoking. Now you do. And of course you're finding that it's much less acceptable, much less popular, shall we say, to be a smoker. And I don't know how much of that is basically political, and how much is apolitical. I don't like the atmosphere today, not only for smoking, but I find that that's true in many other areas of freedom.

Davis: How do you experience it? How do you get that feeling from other people?

Michael: Well, fifteen years ago you didn't think about it. You walked into someone's house and they would offer you an ashtray. You don't do that anymore. I don't even ask anymore, "Is it OK if we smoke?" because for a while there it was, "Well, I really wish you wouldn't."

Davis: And that was awkward?

Michael: No, it wasn't awkward, it's just that you learn not to ask anymore, and just assume that it's not right.

Peggy: I found it awkward.

Michael: You go to parties now. You know, where it used to be that everyone was standing around with a cocktail in one hand and a cigarette in the other and blabbing, and now you see the smokers, kind of, if it's an apartment, furtively standing around an open window, or if it's a house, standing outside in groups. It's pretty common.

Davis: Has it changed your smoking habits in any way?

Peggy: That's hard to say. I will say this: I know that I'm much more cognizant of my surroundings. For example, if I walk into someone else's office anymore, I would never think to take a cigarette. And like he said, in someone's home, you wouldn't automatically sit down and have a cigarette. So in that regard, yes.

Michael: Yeah. I mean, I've developed a whole body language about smoking in groups and in places where it is permissible to smoke.

Peggy: Oh yes.

Michael: It's . . . you take a drag.

Davis: As you're doing right now.

Michael: Right. Blow it straight up in the air so that it doesn't get in anybody's face, then try to hold your cigarette so that the wind catches, whatever wind there is catches it so, that it goes away from the group. So after a while, you look like a factory. You're blowing smoke straight up, and you've got this cigarette flying out in the air there. It's a whole body language.

Peggy: And you do look a bit strange, you're right, now that you say that. Do you feel any defiance?

Michael: I don't think I do. I've never felt a desire to inflict my habit on anybody else.

Peggy: I guess I don't mean inflict your habit. I think when I mean defiance, what I mean by that is, if you are in an area where it is totally acceptable to smoke, that you know that there is someone there who doesn't really want you to smoke.

Michael: Yes, yes. Actually, one afternoon I was coming home from work. I was walking up Connecticut Avenue and I had my Walkman™ on. It had been kind of a rough day, and I was puffing away on a cigarette and walking up the street, and someone came up in front of me and pointed behind me. So I took my Walkman™ off, and turned around, and there was this man standing there, and he was going, "Excuse me, your cigarette is in my eyes."

Peggy: And you were outside.

Michael: I was outside, on the sidewalk. And I looked at him, and I said, "Well, then walk in front of me." And I just felt like he was his own private smoking patrol. It had nothing to do with any kind of physical discomfort I was causing him.

Peggy: And did you wonder if, the next day, he was part of the fur patrol? That's what I think I mean about defiance. I find that in myself, that when they make a judgment, and that's basically what they're doing, they're making a judgment on my behavior.

Davis: Do you understand at all, though, this strong feeling that people have about smoking, that if they're not a smoker, they don't want to be around it, they don't want to inhale the smoke?

Michael: Yes, I can understand it. Sure. I mean, I've really knuckled under. I have changed my habits to respect the rights of people who don't want smoke around them, and I'm much more cognizant of how my smoking might be affecting the general area. If I'm in a smoking section, I feel that I'm entitled to smoke. If they take away that smoking section, I won't smoke in there anymore.

Peggy: I wouldn't go there anymore. If it's a matter of spending my money in a restaurant, for example, I wouldn't spend my money there. But in regard to that, yes, I understand it, but I also feel, again, back to equity. Give me my place to smoke. That's all I ask.

Davis: Peggy and Michael both live in Washington, D.C.

Section 7: Looking at Language

Michael: My name is Michael, and *I've been smoking* for fifteen years.

Peggy: My name's Peggy, and *I've been smoking* for probably thirty to thirty-five years.

Michael: *I've developed* a whole body language about smoking in groups and in places where it is permissible to smoke.

Michael: *I've never felt* a desire to inflict my habit on anybody else.

UNIT 2
A WINE THAT'S RAISED SOME STINK

Introduction: From California comes word of a new wine, a first in the United States, probably the world.

Man: It's not like any wine I've ever had before. There's a taste in here, I can't quite identify it; something I've never associated with wine.

Woman: You can smell the garlic, but I . . . it was a very familiar taste to me as I was tasting it, but I didn't know what it was, and . . . garlic, are they serious?

Lee Thornton: Yes, they are. The winery that created this new Garlic Dinner Wine™ is in Gilroy, California,

and in Gilroy everyone is serious about garlic. It's the garlic capital of the world. The label promises an experience that never leaves you breathless. Co-owner Sandra Rappazini says orders are pouring in for the five-dollars-a-bottle wine, and the company is looking at prospects for national and international marketing campaigns. But why garlic wine?

Rappazini: Well, why not? In fact, last year, just after the fourth Garlic Festival, we sat down and discussed amongst our family staff just in what way the following year that we could contribute to the area and the fact that we live in the garlic capital. So we decided, why not a garlic wine? And then we went ahead and did some experimenting for the entire year and finally derived a formula that allowed us to come up with the wine that we were satisfied with, and voilà, we found out that people loved it.

Thornton: Is it a trade secret now how you make it? Can I ask you what goes into the making of this wine?

Rappazini: Well, I would say it is a secret formula in that, since we spent a year checking the different types of garlic essence or powder or fresh garlic that we might want to use at specific times of fermentation and aging, I would have to say yes, it is kind of a trade secret. Oh, we've had probably more fun so far than we've probably had with any other wine, I will be honest. And I can tell you one other story. I sing with a group called the "Vintage Four" that I have assembled this last year. So we got to laughing one night and decided we would write a song called "The Garlic Song," which we have done.

Thornton: Do you, can you sing any of it?

Rappazini: Sure.

You've heard about the wine
You shouldn't drink before its time.
And you've heard about the wine
That you can drink at any time.
But let us tell you now about a wine
That's raised some stink,
From a little town called Gilroy,
Where garlic is king.
It's Rappazini's garlic wine.
Makes your kissin' sweet
And makes your breath mighty fine.
It's Rapazzini's garlic wine.
Share it with a friend,
And have a mighty fine time.

Man: Ooh, tastes like something you'd put on your salad.

Thornton: Do you like it?

Man: Yeah, it's got a bit of a tang to it, a little bit of bite.

Woman: It's almost got a pungent sort of taste to it.

Thornton: What does it taste like to you?

Woman: Pine Sol™.

Thornton: What would you say to somebody who just could not get past the prejudice of the idea of garlic wine?

Rappazini: First I would try to convince them to taste it along with something that had garlic in the dish or in the cuisine. And secondly, I would, I think, I would try to humor them into it. I think that's what this is all about. It's meant to prove that wine can be fun, that it's not necessarily a stuffy product, that in California we're just beginning to have all the fun that we deserve with the wine industry.

Man: I don't think, personally, I would use it every night. Gosh, garlic wine.

Man: It really does kind of taste like salad dressing.

Woman: It's nice; it's dry.

Man: Where's it from? Are you going to show it to me? "Garlic Dinner Wine™." I was right, it's garlic, great. Now you can explain this to all my colleagues all day long.

Thornton: Volunteer wine tasters at National Public Radio and Sandra Rappazini.

Section 7: Looking at Language

Announcer: Exercise 1.

Song: You've heard about the wine
You shouldn't drink before its time.
And you've heard about the wine
That you can drink at any time.
But let us tell you now about a wine
That's raised some stink,
From a little town called Gilroy,
Where garlic is king.
It's Rappazini's garlic wine.
Makes your kissin' sweet

And makes your breath mighty fine.
It's Rapazzini's garlic wine.
Share it with a friend,
And have a mighty fine time.

UNIT 3
DRIVE-IN SHOPPING

Introduction: In Los Angeles some 1,200 people are doing their weekly grocery shopping in record time without the grocery carts or without the check-out lines. NPR's America Rodriguez prepared this report on a new drive-in supermarket that can accommodate 300 cars an hour.

Man: It's a great time saver. The idea that I can drive up and get my groceries and be on my way in six minutes is fantastic.

Rodriguez: How long does it usually take you at a regular grocery store to do your grocery shopping?

Woman: Oh, at least a couple hours, you know, until then after that you're waiting in line . . . it's a hassle for me; I'm not real big on it.

Rodriguez: Near the intersection of two major Los Angeles freeways is a sign of the times and perhaps of the future: a supermarket where you don't have to fight for a parking space, where you don't have to stand in line, and where you don't even have to get out of your car.

Dave Burstein: We took two proven, successful ideas. One was the success of drive-through convenience—which has been proven to be successful with banks and fast food, and I believe in California we even have drive-through chapels and mortuaries—and then we took the proven success of catalog shopping, applied both of those to the grocery industry.

Rodriguez: Dave Burstein, vice-president for marketing of the Phone-In Drive-Through Market. Butter and broccoli, bubble-bath and birdfood, all are available from this high-tech, fully computerized grocery store. Customers make up their grocery lists from a 4,000-item catalog and then phone in the item numbers.

Woman: OK, can I have your home telephone number?

Rodriguez: Once the order is in, the computer takes over. The computer turns your grocery list into a printout. Workers then follow the numbers through a warehouse. The computer even tells them how to pack the bags, so a can of beans doesn't crush a loaf of bread. Meanwhile you go about your business and, three hours later, drive up to the market, punch your code into a terminal, and write a check while your groceries are loaded into your car.

Burstein: Our pitch is very simple. Our reason for being is to save time. We feel we can get you in and out of here from the time you announce that you're here in less than two minutes.

Man: Hi.

Man: I got your order all ready.

Man: By this time I'd probably get a parking space at another place.

Rodriguez: There *are* disadvantages to this fast-lane grocery shopping. You can't stop and sniff the fish or squeeze the melon. The store stocks only fancy-grade produce and keeps perishable items in freezers or refrigerators until you come and pick them up. I heard no complaints about the freshness of the food. And you pay a $1.50 service charge on each order, but prices are comparable to traditional grocery stores. And as one customer put it, "My time is worth more than a dollar-and-a-half an hour."

Woman: I phone in the order from work, and on my way home I can pick it up. It's an idea whose time has really come. I've been wondering for a long time why I can't order groceries more efficiently. There seems no reason to have so many bodies walking around a grocery store.

Woman: I'm sure it's the new and incoming way of doing things in the future.

Rodriguez: If the idea of a drive-through supermarket catches on—and it's now doing better than expected—its owners hope to franchise phone-in, drive-through markets throughout the country and someday hook up grocery store computers to home computers and two-way TV sets.

Man: I don't have any hours left in the day, so it's kind of fun while you're watching TV to fill out your grocery order, and then it just takes a few minutes.

Man: Can you believe it's a grocery store?

Rodriguez: I'm America Rodriguez in Los Angeles.

Section 7: Looking at Language

Rodriguez: There *are* disadvantages to this fast-lane grocery shopping. You can't stop and sniff the fish or squeeze the melon.

UNIT 4
IS IT A SCULPTURE, OR IS IT FOOD?

Noah Adams: In the near future, you might be able to buy a tomato in the supermarket that has been genetically designed and engineered, a tomato that would stay ripe much longer, strawberries that are not so fragile in freezing temperatures, vegetable oil that's lower in fat. Already on the market: a gene-spliced product that's used in cheese making. There are impressive claims being made for genetic manipulation of food, including production increases that could help alleviate world hunger. But there's also concern, and indeed some fear, about the use of gene-splicing techniques, and last week more than 1,000 chefs from restaurants all around the country made a pledge they will not serve such foods, and they'll work to see that genetically engineered foods are labeled as such. It was announced back in May that no special labeling would be required. Joyce Goldstein has joined the boycott. She's the owner of Square One Restaurant in San Francisco.

Goldstein: When I first heard about it, I thought, Well, they're not even talking about flavor. The only thing they're talking about is how long they can keep the damn thing on the shelf.

Adams: You're talking about the tomato, basically.

Goldstein: Basically the tomato. You know, you worry how long they want to keep it. Is it a sculpture, or is it food? And I just kept thinking, I hope that we will get to find out more about this, and that they'll do some testing. For example, if they're using these trout genes in other products, and we have customers with fish allergies, are they going to get sick?

Adams: There's the idea that they would use a fish gene to make tomatoes more frost-resistant.

Goldstein: Right. Well, I mean, will people with fish allergies have responses to this, or will that be so sublimated that they won't have any effect? I guess the thing is, when a new product comes on the market like this, number one, you'd like to be aware that it's being sold to you, and number two, you'd like to know that they have checked out all of these ramifications before they put it on the shelf.

Adams: It sounds like your concerns are more practical than others'. Other people are talking about science fiction food; and I've heard it referred to as "Frankenfood" in the past.

Goldstein: Well, you know, it's very easy to poke fun at—and I want to put this in quotes—"progress." I mean, those of us that were attached to typewriters, I think, poked fun at people using computers until we started using them. So I don't want to sound like I'm some old fogey saying, "In the old days we didn't do it that way." If they could come up with a wonderful product through genetic—I mean, they have done wonderful roses with genetic breeding that are perfectly beautiful and still have some scent—if they could do this and prove it was safe to the public, I'm not going to say it's a bad thing. All I'm saying is, right now we have a lot of nonknowledge about this stuff, and until things are tested and until we know what they taste like and how they are, we don't want to put them on the menu.

Adams: There's an argument that's being made that this could be, I've seen one quotation, "the biggest boon to corporate profits since frozen food," that this could be that big a breakthrough in the food area.

Goldstein: Well, they're always worrying about corporate profit. What if the stuff turns out not to be good? I got a letter from a lady the other day, who said she's the wife of a scientist, and she would prefer to serve genetically engineered food to her children, and I shouldn't worry because it's under the wonderful eye of the Food and Drug Administration, and she will boycott my restaurant as long as I boycott these foods. And I started thinking, God, with an attitude like that I certainly don't want her eating in my restaurant anyway. But also, I mean the Food and Drug Administration has not been foolproof. I think we just need to see a little bit more data on this, and I think it's too soon to tell.

Adams: Now you're very concerned, I'm sure, about pesticide residue in the foods you do serve.

Goldstein: Yes, I am.

Adams: Conceivably, in the future, you could put a gene into some of the foods that would reduce the dependence on pesticides in the field.

Goldstein: I think that's a good thing. I'm just concerned when they start crossing trout with tomatoes as to what happens. I'm concerned. I will be delighted if they can make something taste wonderful and not have chemicals and pesticides. When you read that these things are

happening, and you know that the first person that it's good for is agribusiness, and then you wonder, Well, how good is it for the consumer, and that they will put these things at the market or try to sell it to us without letting us know, I think we have the right to know. I think then we have the choice to say I'm going to buy it, or I'm not going to.

Adams: Joyce Goldstein, the owner and head chef of Square One Restaurant in San Francisco.

Section 7: Looking at Language

Adams: In the near future, you might be able to buy a tomato in the supermarket that has been genetically designed and engineered, a tomato that would stay ripe much longer, strawberries that are not so fragile in freezing temperatures, vegetable oil that's lower in fat. Already on the market, a gene-spliced product that's used in cheese making. There are impressive claims being made for genetic manipulation of food, including production increases that could help alleviate world hunger. But there's also concern, and indeed some fear, about the use of gene-splicing techniques. . . .

UNIT 5
GANG VIOLENCE

Nina Totenberg: In 1983 in Chicago at least seventy-five murders were attributed to street-gang violence; that's 10 percent of all the murders reported in the city. There are more than 100 gangs in the city. Membership varies from 10 to 4,000. Almost all of the gang members are under the age of twenty. Nathaniel Shepard and William Recktenwald are reporting on gang violence in Chicago and its suburbs for *The Chicago Tribune* this week. I asked Recktenwald, Who joins these exclusively male gangs?

Recktenwald: These are individuals that are afraid to stand alone. They're generally cowards. They go out at night, and they do things at night. They don't fight one on one; it's always six or seven people that sneak up and ambush people or shoot at people. And we saw a very shocking example yesterday afternoon on the city's south side, where six members of one gang were chasing two members of another gang—right there the odds aren't very even—and suddenly, one of the two being chased turns around with a handgun and starts firing at the six people chasing him. Well, they ducked, but unfortunately there was a twelve-year-old boy standing in the street that was struck three times in the back and killed.

Totenberg: What's the reason for these gangs, and how do they operate, and why do they operate?

Recktenwald: I've talked to a lot of people including a lot of gang members. Perhaps they're looking for some identity; perhaps it makes them feel big and tough. But they take a look at the local pimp or the local drug dealer and see that he seems to be doing well—driving his big car, wearing his fur coat, whatever—and they think, Well, gee, you know, this is what I want to be; I want to make lots of money. And because of that, they'll end up getting involved in a gang. Gangs. Their prime livelihood is through drug and narcotic sales.

Totenberg: You described some of the rituals of the gangs that have led to innocent people being victimized. Would you tell us some of those things?

Recktenwald: Well, there's a whole system of what's called signaling your group affiliation, or what they call representing, that you're representing your affiliation with a particular group. And that goes from hand signals which, when the hand signal is given upwards, it means you're a member of the gang, when it's, when the hand signal is reversed and given downwards, it means death to the gang. And some of these kids lack the maturity of anyone that has good sense, and they turn around and they see a person put the hand signals down for their gang, and they won't go over and punch the person in the nose. They'll pull out a gun and shoot and kill the person. And the lack of remorse is what I think characterizes these members that are in gangs.

Totenberg: How many people are we talking about? How big an area of Chicago? Is there any way to control this situation?

Recktenwald: This is, surprisingly enough, an area that I think we can control much easier than many of our problems in society. We're talking about generally here a lack of control of young people by their parents. So, you control . . . you know, you get parents to control their kids.

Totenberg: But, Bill, you're talking about, probably in most cases, families that are very fragile or nonexistent. That's why these kids are in this situation. I mean, you can't just press a button and say, "Well, families, be responsible."

Recktenwald: Well, it's a team effort. You take the community also; if the community stands up they can push the gangs out, because there's more good people in this city than there are gang members.

Totenberg: What specifically . . . what does the community do?

Recktenwald: Well, you start out perhaps with a block club. You start out with a graffiti watch. You have telephone chains, where if you look our your front window and you see a group of kids involved in something they shouldn't be, that you pick up your telephone and you call the police. And in addition to calling the police, you call your next-door neighbor and have him or her look out the front window, see what's happening and have them pick up the phone and call the police. And then they should call the next next-door neighbor and they look out the window and see what happened and then they call the police. And when the police come, the neighbors volunteer to be witnesses and appear in court, and when the charges are pressed, they go down to court and let that judge know that neighborhood's interested in what's going on.

Section 7: Looking at Language

Recktenwald: This is, surprisingly enough, an area that I think we can control much easier than many of our problems in society. We're talking about generally here a lack of control of young people by their parents. So, you control . . . you know, you get parents to control their kids.

Totenberg: But, Bill, you're talking about, probably in most cases, families that are very fragile or nonexistent. That's why these kids are in this situation. I mean, you can't just press a button and say, "Well, families, be responsible."

UNIT 6
CREATE CONTROVERSY TO GENERATE PUBLICITY

Linda Wertheimer: Benetton has produced a set of controversial ads which, even in these hard times for advertising revenues, magazines are turning down. The three controversial ads depict a very young nun kissing a priest, a newborn baby only seconds old, and a little blonde white girl next to a little black boy whose hair is fashioned into something that looks a little bit like horns. Our own Bob Garfield, in his other life, is the advertising critic for *Advertising Age* magazine, and since he has opinions about practically everything, and professionally he has opinions about advertising, we called him.

Bob, what about these ads? What do nuns and priests and newborns and little toddlers blonde and black have to do with selling T-shirts?

Garfield: Well, they have everything to do with us doing this interview right now. An important element of this whole campaign is to create controversy and to generate publicity, which not only has an immediate value all of its own, it also enhances every consumer exposure to Benetton ads in their natural habitat, so that when you're paging through some magazine and run across a picture of this newborn baby covered with the blood and the vernix and with the umbilicus still attached, instead of casually passing it, being aware of the controversy, you're apt to look at it more seriously and to react one way or another—probably with anger or disgust, is my guess.

Wertheimer: I think that if you . . . uh . . . if you were paging through a magazine and saw this picture, you would stop cold, even if you'd never heard of the ad or Benetton, because it is such an arresting picture, this baby.

Garfield: Well it is that, . . . uh, arresting, some would say disgusting. And I suppose the Benetton people would say that it's magnificent and natural. But I think a large intestine is natural and kind of magnificent in its way, but I sure don't want to see it in the middle of a fashion magazine, though I suppose that's next.

Wertheimer: *Essence* and *Child* magazine did not take the ad with the two children; *Self*, which published the baby, refused the nun; *Cosmopolitan* decided it did not see itself with a newborn baby in its pages. Now, were you suprised? I mean, I'm surprised by that. This is a double page ad, and magazines are awfully skinny; it seems to me they're being awfully touchy about it.

Garfield: Oh, I don't know if awfully touchy is right. I mean, I frankly don't think Benetton really expected these ads to be accepted by anyone. I'm a little surprised that the newborn one was in the pages of *Self*. These ads were created for the express purpose of ticking people off, for creating controversy, for inflaming consumer outrage, and so forth and so on, and it's really very cunning advertising, Linda, for a lot of reasons. Not only is there the publicity benefit, they also are a great example of what I call distraction marketing. And it's distracting, because, rather than focus on trying to come up with some sort of rational benefit for buying a forty-nine-dol-

lar cotton T-shirt, which Benetton knows is not a rational kind of consumer behavior, they're kind of playing a little three-card monte in creating a distraction over here so you won't pay attention to the facts of the matter over on the other side, the facts of the matter being that a $119 cardigan sweater is not a particularly good buy.

Wertheimer: Thanks very much.

Garfield: My pleasure.

Wertheimer: Bob Garfield, when he is not appearing on National Public Radio, is the advertising critic for *Advertising Age*.

Section 7: Looking at Language

Announcer: Number 1.

Wertheimer: I think that if you . . . uh . . . if you were paging through a magazine and you saw this picture, you would stop cold . . . even if you'd never heard of the ad or Benetton . . . because it is such an *arresting* picture, this baby.

Announcer: Number 2.

Garfield: Well, it is that . . . uh, arresting, some would say *disgusting*. And I suppose the Benetton people would say that it's *magnificent* and *natural*.

Announcer: Number 3.

Garfield: It's really very *cunning* advertising, Linda, for a lot of reasons.

Announcer: Number 4.

Garfield: It's distracting, because, rather than focus on trying to come up with some sort of rational benefit for buying a forty-nine dollar cotton T-shirt, which Benetton knows is not a rational kind of consumer behavior, they're kind of playing a little three-card monte in creating a distraction over here so you won't pay attention to the facts of the matter over on the other side, the facts of the matter being that a $119 cardigan sweater is not a particularly good buy.

UNIT 7
WOMEN CAUGHT IN THE MIDDLE OF TWO GENERATIONS

Introduction: This is "Morning Edition"; I'm Bob Edwards. There are now 26.5 million Americans age sixty-five and older. The vast majority have children, many of whom are involved in their parents' old age. The reason is those children—usually daughters and daughters-in-law—have become caretakers of the old. They may help parents to live independently or take them into their own homes. Today in our series on women and the issues affecting them, a report prepared by NPR's Katherine Ferguson on three caretakers.

Susan: My husband would go to work and I had my mother-in-law.

Margaret: It was just taking up more and more of my time, and I was becoming just a full-time sitter for my mother. And she would fall and break a hip, or another bone, and I would have to go flying off to take care of her.

Ferguson: All three women, who live in Charlottesville, Virginia, qualify as caretakers of aging parents. More and more middle-aged adults are finding themselves in the position of caring for parents. There are more older Americans than ever before; parents are living longer, and smaller families mean there are fewer children to share the responsibilities. Susan and her husband had not made plans for a time when his mother would be unable to live alone. When illness made Susan's mother-in-law blind, bringing her to live with them seemed the only choice.

Susan: When she came, she actually became my constant companion. I took her with me when we went to the grocery store; I took her with me shopping. I took her with me everyplace.

Ferguson: The situation was much the same for Vivian—no plans had been made for her mother's care. Vivian, like Susan, had never worked outside the home. When her mother moved in, her full-time job became caretaking. She found her days defined by her mother's needs and desires—breakfast in bed at 8:30, a morning walk, an afternoon drive, evening television viewing. Vivian felt she could only be away from home for short periods, because her mother needed constant reassurance.

Vivian: When I was asked for the tenth time that morning what time I was coming home from going shopping, I would just really have to say, "For God's sake, I told you that ten times already; I'll be back in time to fix your lunch."

Ferguson: Seven days a week, fifty-two weeks a year for five years, the strain of full-time caretaking takes its toll on loving daughters and their family. After repeat-edly babysitting his grandmother, Vivian's son finally said he no longer enjoyed coming home. Susan and her husband found the constant lack of privacy placed stress on their marriage.

Susan: How can you explain it to them: I want to fight with my husband, you're sitting there, please go away. I mean you can't say these things.

Ferguson: Not expressing the anger and resentment was the hardest part of caretaking for Susan and Vivian, and it was in large measure the reason they sought out other women in the same predicament. They joined a support group for caretakers, where they could talk about their sense of duty, that they should be caring for parents, and to share their shame at resenting it. Susan is still angry about losing control of her life.

Susan: You want to take care of them, but the process of caring for them makes you trapped. Your whole life is changed.

Ferguson: Until recently Margaret's mother lived across the country in Arizona. So Margaret didn't experience a feeling of being trapped by daily schedules, but periodically her mother would become ill.

Margaret: Oh, I would go for a year-and-a-half and nothing would happen. And then there'd be a six-month period where I'd have to tear off to take care of her.

Ferguson: Margaret's transcontinental caretaking ended when her mother came to Charlottesville. And in caring for a brain-damaged parent, Margaret experienced what many others found: Roles reversed when daughters care for dependent mothers.

Margaret: It's like having a retarded child to care for.

Ferguson: Vivian's mother began introducing her daughter as "my mother."

Vivian: To suddenly be put in the mother role again and be faced with perhaps another five or ten years of being a mother again to my own mother—I simply didn't want to do it. And I was tired of being a mother; I wanted to be something else.

Ferguson: Susan, Margaret, and Vivian are among those now described as women caught in the middle of two generations. Their children are grown when once again they're called on to mother. It's a role they don't expect and aren't happy about resuming. These three women have now placed their mothers in nursing homes. For Susan and Margaret, medical considerations made the decision for them. The situation was not so clear-cut for Vivian. In the end, her children helped her overcome the guilt.

Vivian: Should I do this to my own mother? After all, she's my mother. I can't very well just pick her up and transplant her to a nursing home. And yes, they said, "Yes you can, and in the long run she'll be happier, and you will too."

Ferguson: These families are lucky. They can handle the cost of nursing-home care. But even when finances are not a major consideration, there's the emotional price to pay for having a parent in a nursing home.

Vivian: And it scares you; you can see yourself in somebody like that. And it's not easy to face it.

Ferguson: Caring for aging parents has helped these three women face their own old age. They now want to plan for the future. None of them want to live with their children when they're no longer able to care for themselves. Being in a nursing home seems preferable to asking their own children to become caretakers.

Section 7: Looking at Language

Susan: My husband would go to work and I had my mother-in-law.

Margaret: It was just taking up more and more of my time, and I was becoming just a full-time sitter for my mother. And she would fall and break a hip, or another bone, and I would have to go flying off to take care of her.

UNIT 8:
THE MAIL-ORDER BRIDE

Introduction: Most of us think the mail-order bride went the way of the stagecoach. She did, for a while. Now she's back, this time in cross-cultural form. In the past decade, the number of visas issued to Asians coming to this country to marry Americans has jumped from 34 to 3,400, and the number of mail-order-bride services has quadrupled. Louis Florence and his wife, Tessie, have operated their American Asian Worldwide Service since 1979. They claim to have arranged more than 750 marriages. For about $360 a man can correspond exclusively with many women from a whole catalog of candidates. Louis Florence says his customers are men who are disillusioned by American women.

Louis Florence: They are turned off, they say, because of the lack of femininity, but once they're married all the love and romance goes out of the marriage. It's been our experience from talking to these gentlemen—these gentlemen have been married four, five years now—that once they are married to these ladies from the Philippines and Malaysia, it's as though they're on their honeymoon right now.

Lee Thornton: You've made the allusion—you seem to give the impression that you might believe that Asian women have a corner on these attributes, if that's what they are, of knowing how to please. Is that what you're saying?

Louis Florence: Well, from my personal experience, being married to lovely Tess, she has been brought up in the Asian culture that makes her feel as though . . . that she will love, honor, obey, and treat her husband very nicely all the time.

Thornton: This is all coming out in kind of one direction. I wonder if there are any controls on this. Are there protections, for example, for the women once they're here?

Louis Florence: Before the girls even come over here, we conduct a personality evaluation. This is a questionnaire that we send the ladies that has over 200 questions, 600 possible answers. It asks the type of questions that no man would ever ask a gal that he met at the local church or his local disco. The girls must complete this and get it certified and notarized. Now, as time progresses, and one of our clients chooses one of these ladies, we volunteer to have Tess talk to the lady. We take and go through great lengths to instruct our clients what to expect.

Thornton: That personality evaluation profile that you mentioned, who wrote it?

Louis Florence: Tess did. She wrote it, designed it, and came up with the complete analysis system for it.

Thornton: Tessie Florence.

Tessie Florence.   Hi. Yes.

Thornton: I'd like to ask you how you made up this form, this personality profile, this evaluation.

Tessie Florence: There are some questions that most of the gentlemen cannot afford to ask the ladies. So I thought of devising those questions for our clients to submit it with their form. Because—

Thornton: What are some of those questions that the gentlemen can't afford to ask? I'm looking at it now. Here's a question: "Do you polish your toenails?"

Tessie Florence: There are some clients who don't want to correspond with ladies who are polishing their nails, toenails, who are wearing makeups. They just want the traditional type of lady.

Thornton: Well, now, here's another question: "What size breasts do you have?" Is that a major question?

Tessie Florence: Yes, that's part of the sexuality, and that particular question he cannot afford to ask the lady.

Thornton: You know, Mr. Florence, critics of operations, companies, businesses such as yours say you are peddling flesh. How would you respond to that?

Louis Florence: I violently disagree. We offer an alternative to the common methods of meeting somebody of the opposite sex. Here in the United States you can go to a disco, you can go to a singles bar—which, as far as I'm concerned, are flesh markets. You can go to church, or you can sit down and go through our catalogs or run an ad and get letters from ladies. And sit there without physically and personally trying to touch her and sit and pour your heart out and write letters and get to know each other by correspondence. And our marriages, we find, are working out.

Thornton: Louis and Tessie Florence, operators of the American Asian Worldwide Service.

Section 7: Looking at Language

Announcer: Exercise 1. Number 1.

Introduction: Most of us think the mail-order bride went the way of the stagecoach. She did, for a while. Now she's back, this time in cross-cultural form.

Announcer: Number 2.

Thornton: Louis Florence says his customers are men who are disillusioned by American women.

Louis Florence: They are turned off, they say, because of the lack of femininity.

Announcer: Number 3.

Thornton: You've made the allusion—you seem to give the impression that you might believe that Asian women have a corner on these attributes, if that's what they are, of knowing how to please. Is that what you're saying?

Louis Florence: Well, from my personal experience, being married to lovely Tess, she has been brought up in the Asian culture that makes her feel as though . . . that she will love, honor, obey, and treat her husband very nicely all the time.

Announcer: Number 4.

Tessie Florence: There are some questions that most of the gentlemen cannot afford to ask the ladies. So I thought of devising those questions for our clients to submit it with their form.

Announcer: Number 5.

Thornton: You know, Mr. Florence, critics of operations, companies, businesses such as yours say you are peddling flesh. How would you respond to that?

Louis Florence: I violently disagree. We offer an alternative to the common methods of meeting somebody of the opposite sex.

Announcer: Number 6.

Louis Florence: Here in the United States you can go to a disco, you can go to a singles bar—which, as far as I'm concerned, are flesh markets. You can go to church, or you can sit down and go through our catalogs or run an ad and get letters from ladies. And sit there without physically and personally trying to touch her and sit and pour your heart out and write letters and get to know each other by correspondence.

Announcer: Number 7.

Louis Florence: And our marriages, we find, are working out.

UNIT 9:
FACING THE WRONG END OF A PISTOL

Introduction: Handguns account for much of the violent crime in this country. Statistics show that one out of every five of us will face the wrong end of a pistol in our lives. The Senate Judiciary Committee decided this week to propose changes in the 1968 Gun Control Act that would lift most bans against the sales of guns across state lines. During the debate Sen. Edward Kennedy tried, but failed, to exempt the guns known as "Saturday Night Specials" from the proposal. Olen Kelley, a grocery store manager from Silver Spring, Maryland, has launched his own attack against Saturday Night Specials.

He's filed suit in his home county's circuit court to try to stop the manufacture and distribution of the cheap handguns. Kelley has been held up more than once; each time the robber had a gun. A year ago he was held up for the fifth time by two men who were after the money in the store's safe.

Kelley: And I missed the combination the first time. So one of 'em, with the gun, put the gun up to the side of my head, pulled the hammer back and said, "Uh, don't miss it a second time." So, I slowed down, made sure I got the safe open, and then they told me to lay down on the floor. Well, after I lay down on the floor, they . . . one of them hit me over the head with something. It probably was his fist, I'm not sure; and the other one shot me.

Breeding: He shot you?

Kelley: Yes.

Breeding: Did he injure you badly?

Kelley: He shot me in the shoulder. It came out my armpit, went back in my armpit, traveled down my side, and came out the lower part of my side.

Breeding: How about the other times that you were attacked? Were they also with guns?

Kelley: Handguns, yes.

Breeding: Who are you suing, then?

Kelley: I'm suing the distributor of this particular gun, what is the name of the company. . . . The name of the gun is a Relm. The distributor is in Florida, and the maker of the gun is in Germany. I don't know all the legal technicalities to do this, but I feel that these people that make these guns and distribute them throughout the country should repay for what they're doing.

Breeding: There would be some people who would say to you that, if you had been robbed at knifepoint, say, rather than gunpoint, would you then want to sue the knife manufacturer?

Kelley: Well, the knife manufacturers, just like rifle manufacturers, they're not meant to be such an item as to be used in a crime. They are used that way, granted, but in most incidences you'll find that cheap handguns are used, and used to kill people with. Now a knife is used . . . has other purposes, and that's what it's made for. I'm not after the NRA or I'm not after sporting-type guns. I'm after these particular junk guns—they are of no use to society. And if you probably tried to shoot one of them at a good distance, you probably couldn't hit any-

thing with it anyway. Up close you could, but—and in my instance the guy was about a foot-and-a-half away from me when he shot me.

Breeding: This is likely to be a controversial case. Are you prepared to take it for years and years, you know, all the way to the Supreme Court if you have to?

Kelley: If I have to, yes. Cost me a lot of time, but I'm willing to try. I have to try. I feel I have the right to try.

Breeding: Olen Kelley's suit asks $500 million damages from RG Industries. His lawyers say they hope that, with that award, to make it impossible for the company to make the guns.

Section 7: Looking at Language

Announcer: Exercise 1.

Kelley: And I missed the combination the first time. So one of 'em, with the gun, put the gun up to the side of my head, pulled the hammer back and said, "Uh, don't miss it a second time." So, I slowed down, made sure I got the safe open, and then they told me to lay down on the floor. Well, after I lay down on the floor, they . . . one of them hit me over the head with something. It probably was his fist, I'm not sure; and the other one shot me.

Announcer: Exercise 2.

Breeding: He shot you?

Kelley: Yes.

Breeding: Did he injure you badly?

Kelley: He shot me in the shoulder. It came out my armpit, went back in my armpit, traveled down my side, and came out the lower part of my side.

UNIT 10:
WHAT CONSTITUTES A FAMILY?

Introduction: The traditional family, a wage-earning father and a wife who stays home to take care of the kids, is a disappearing species in this country. The U.S. Census Bureau estimates that just 50 percent of American families fit this profile. But many of the nation's institutions don't recognize the growing ranks of non-traditional groups who are living together: gay couples, foster parents, and stepfamilies. Now California has become the first state in the nation to publicly register these non-traditional groups as official families. Kitty Felde of station KLON in Los Angeles reports.

Felde: Shannon Gibson is like a lot of sixth-graders. She has a mouth full of braces, and she has two fathers: the one she visits every other weekend, and her mother's new husband, Pat Howard. Shannon says she worries about her stepfather's visitation rights if her mother were to die.

Shannon Gibson: Pat is not my biological father, but he's raised me since I was two years old. So it wouldn't be right . . . that I wouldn't be able to see him or anything like that.

Felde: To guarantee that Shannon's extended family will be recognized by the outside world, the Howards have registered with California's secretary of state as a family. For a ten-dollar fee, any group of people can qualify for family status just by filling out a form. This might include stepfamilies, like the Howards, couples of the same sex; even unrelated seniors, like TV's "Golden Girls," who choose to live together for economic reasons but consider themselves a family. A private agency, the Family Diversity Project, championed the family registration concept in California. Executive Director Thomas Coleman says California isn't the only state grappling with the question of what constitutes a family.

Coleman: It was about a year-and-a-half ago that the New York Court of Appeals recognized in a housing survivor case that you can't evict a surviving family member from a rent-controlled apartment, even if they're not related by blood, marriage, or adoption. And unfortunately, what happens then is that you get into all these matters of proof. Well, how do you distinguish a family from a nonfamily? Then the court set up criteria. This is an ongoing process that will probably take at least another ten years to really play out fully.

Felde: California state law allows labor unions, historical societies, or any other association to register their names. Coleman reasoned: Because a family is also an association, they could also register. The secretary of state agreed. Several other states—Oregon, Wisconsin, New Jersey, Virginia, and West Virginia—have registration procedures similar to those in California. But they have not yet registered a family.

The certificate itself carries no automatic legal benefits, but John Brown says it could help legitimize his status as a single father. Brown is legal guardian to four teenage boys. His health insurance covers them, and he legally claims them on his tax return as dependents. But that could change when the oldest starts college next year.

Brown: Just like any parent, I'm going to keep claiming him as a dependent, I'm going to keep him covered on insurance, and if somebody messes with that, I'll use anything I have at my disposal to prove that yes, he is my dependent and yes, I am his parent and we are a family.

Felde: It's likely both the Internal Revenue Service and insurance companies would challenge Brown's family certificate, but backers of the project say registration is an important first step in helping nontraditional families gain acceptance. For National Public Radio, this is Kitty Felde in Los Angeles.

Section 7: Looking at Language

Shannon: Pat is not my biological father, but he's raised me since I was two years old. So it *wouldn't be* right . . . that I *wouldn't be able* to see him or anything like that.

UNIT 11:
FINDING DISCRIMINATION WHERE ONE WOULD HOPE TO FIND RELIEF

Lynn Neary: In addition to the health problems brought on by AIDS, many people who have the disease or have tested positive for the virus that causes it face another painful difficulty: discrimination. And a report released today shows that AIDS discrimination exists even in settings where victims of discrimination might hope to find some relief: the nation's courtrooms and insurance companies. According to the study, released by the National AIDS Program Office, judicial decisions often reinforce myths about how AIDS is transmitted. Larry Gosten, one of the authors of the report, says judges frequently rule that actions such as spitting or biting are serious crimes when the accused has AIDS and often hand down unduly harsh sentences as a result.

Gosten: The surprising thing is that, of over 200 cases, many of which have involved very, very severe criminal penalties, there's no case that I'm aware of where HIV was actually transmitted. We're really convicting people because of the irrational fear that it might be.

Neary: What about the question, though, of intent on the part of the person who actually may have bit somebody and may have felt that by doing that they were inflicting some kind of harm?

Gosten: Well, I think that's the issue that the courts focus on, but it seems to me that you can't really punish somebody for something that's impossible. And in addition, many of these things are cries for help. One case that I remember went all the way up to the Indiana Supreme Court, where a person tried to commit suicide and was unconscious and face down in a pool of blood when health care workers and police came. And they tried to revive him, and his first words were: "Let me die. I have AIDS." And they didn't, of course, bravely, and then he got up and he splattered his blood and said, "I want you to know what it's like to have AIDS." Now that was really a cry for help, but he got four life sentences for that and will, of course, die in prison.

Neary: And what about the problems of people with AIDS, or who have tested positive for HIV, have when they're trying to get insurance, either health insurance or life insurance?

Gosten: Although the public has learned that there are lots of new treatments for AIDS, the fact is that our study shows that many people can't afford the treatments and insurance companies won't insure them. One particular case that troubles me was a federal court of appeals case where an employer found out that their employee had AIDS and then changed the health care benefits, so that instead of giving $1 million coverage for a chronic disease, persons with AIDS, that is, him, could only get $5,000 worth of coverage, and the federal court of appeals upheld it.

Neary: This is a discrimination that springs from a very deep place, I think, inside of people, and that is, their own fear of getting the disease and of dying, because it is a fatal disease.

Gosten: Yes, I think that the fact that it is potentially transmissible . . . somehow people want to have a zero risk, and you can never assure somebody that there is a zero risk. But we're also finding that the discrimination is stemming from economics as well as fear. Lots of people are saying, "Well I'm not prejudiced anymore, but I can't hire this person because my clients won't come," say, if I'm a food handler. Or, they're saying that "It's going to overburden my health benefits plan, and so I won't hire that person." Or in the health care system, they say, "Well, it's not that I'm prejudiced, it's just that I really don't have the clinical expertise to handle this person." These are all veiled forms of discrimination, but they're discrimination nonetheless.

Neary: And yet some would argue very legitimate excuses on each person's behalf.

Gosten: I always like to look at AIDS discrimination like you would look at racial discrimination. It used to be legitimate for somebody to say, "Well, I won't serve an African-American in my restaurant." Well, the courts and society see that as being invidious and repugnant discrimination, and I think we should see that here. We all have to do the right thing. Everybody's entitled to a job if they can do the work. Everybody's entitled to health care if they're ill and they can benefit from it. And we can't say that there are some people, because they have a particular disease, that it's all right for us to exclude them from everyday life. That's sentencing them to something even worse than the terminal illness they have.

Neary: Larry Gosten is executive director of American Society of Law and Medicine.

UNIT 12:
GREEN CONSUMERISM

Steve Curwood: In the last couple of years, bookstore shelves have been flooded with "green" shopping guides. *The Green Consumer. Shopping for a Better World. Fifty Simple Things You Can Do to Save the Planet.* The books are all part of an effort to broaden the environmental movement and bring ecological concerns into our most ordinary daily decisions. But some environmental watchdogs warn that consumers could be lulled into a false complacency by merely shopping differently. To explore the promises and pitfalls of "green consuming," I spoke with Alan Durning, a senior researcher with the World Watch Institute in Washington, D.C., and Alice Tepper Marlin, president of the Council on Economic Priorities, authors of *Shopping for a Better World.*

Tepper Marlin: The number one thing all of us can do to help the environment is to consume less, and to grow ourselves what we need to consume, and put in a compost heap whatever we have left over. But most of us do end up going shopping either at supermarkets, as well as department stores, every once in a while at least, and when we do, it's a good opportunity to turn your shopping cart into a vehicle for social change, by looking for the products that themselves are least harmful for the environment.

Curwood: What about this, Alan Durning? Does this make sense to you?

Durning: In general, I think it's a great idea. But in the long term, it's a first step, and as long as we only think of it as a first step, I'm entirely supportive of it. The longer-term issues, though, are overconsumption. The roughly one billion people who live in advanced industrial countries are responsible for an overwhelming majority of the world's environmental problems; whether it's greenhouse effect or ozone depletion, even deforestation, we at the top are the problem, and we can't consume our way out of this. We have got to shift our emphasis away from gross consumption of things to a more, maybe, subtle lifestyle.

Curwood: So on the one hand, one could say that green consuming is a bit like, what's the line, rearranging those deck chairs on the *Titanic* a bit. Or, do you think this is a vehicle for raising people's consciousness?

Durning: Well, I think that it really is an initial educational step, and I fully support it in that way. But I think that we have to, at the same time, be critical of the corporations that make use of this kind of rhetoric in their advertising to make themselves seem green. There's a lot of "greenwash" going on. Most recently, I saw an ad from Texaco where they said if you fill your tank, they'll give you a tree seedling. You have to buy at least eight gallons per fill-up if you want to get the tree seedling, and then you can go plant it somewhere to make the world a greener place. But that's the most absurd and ridiculous thing I've ever seen. Planting a tree seedling, which will first of all probably die, is never going to make up for the full tank of gasoline that you burned in order to get that tree seedling. So we have to be very leery about the green marketing that's going on right now.

Curwood: Now what about this, Alice Tepper Marlin? Isn't there a lot of hustle out there, "ecohustle," in the market?

Tepper Marlin: Well, there's no question there are a lot of hucksters out there in all areas. There are hucksters telling us things are safe when they're not, there are hucksters telling children that they should eat candy as breakfast cereals, and there are lots of hucksters out there right now on the green consumer bandwagon, because that's the hot new issue for the nineties. That doesn't mean, however, that one has to throw out the entire concept. It means that consumers need to be well informed, and preferably that there are guidelines, enforced regulations on the federal level, which define what labels on the package and in advertising mean in the green area.

Curwood: It seems to me that the green consuming movement could get people just sort of feeling good about what they're doing and not taking the important

steps that they need to take. Is that fair to say?

Durning: There's a definite risk that it'll make Yuppies feel they have clean hands, they don't have to worry about the environment because they're doing their part by recycling bottles and recycling newspapers, but not really addressing their basic lifestyle questions. The advertisers are playing up to this in what I consider a very cynical way. Toyota recently has run a major series of ads. They flash something across the screen that says, "New Values," and then they talk about how excess is out and recycling and friends and community are in. And then at the conclusion of this, this sort of perverse logic is, we may not have all the answers, but we know which car to buy. Now that's absurd. The point is that you shouldn't buy a car. Cars are one of the most damaging artifacts of modern civilization. And sure, it's better to buy a fuel-efficient, small car than a big one, but really we should be thinking about reforming our transportation systems, about revitalizing public transportation, about revitalizing rail transportation. So there's a definite risk that this will make us feel better than we really are. But it's a risk that we have to take. It's a strategy for social change that's got to be used. We've got to use every strategy, and really, during the 1980s we in the environmental movement missed out on all the millions of people who really would like to do little things. They do make quite a difference.

Curwood: Alan Durning is a senior researcher with the World Watch Institute in Washington, D.C., and Alice Tepper Marlin is the president of the Council on Economic Priorities in New York City.

Section 7: Looking at Language

Announcer: Number 1.

Curwood: It seems to me that the green consuming movement could get people just sort of feeling good about what they're doing. . . .

Announcer: Number 2.

Durning: So there's a definite risk that this will *make* us *feel* better than we really are. But it's a risk that we have to take.

ANSWER KEY

UNIT 1

Give Me My Place to Smoke!

3. VOCABULARY
1. double 2. politically involved 3. after-dinner drink 4. lecturing 5. openly 6. intelligent 7. pull 8. relief 9. soften 10. patron 11. fight

4. TASK LISTENING
Michael is.

5. LISTENING FOR MAIN IDEAS
Suggested answers:
Part 1: The public's attitude toward smokers has changed over the years.
Part 2: Today smokers don't even ask to smoke in other people's homes.

Part 3: Smokers have started smoking so that their smoke won't bother other people.
Part 4: Smokers sometimes feel defiant when they smoke in a smoking area where nonsmokers judge them negatively.
Part 5: Michael respects nonsmoking sections, whereas Peggy won't go to public places that prohibit smoking.

6. LISTENING FOR DETAILS
Part 1: 1. F 2. T 3. T 4. F 5. F 6. T
Part 2: 7. T 8. F 9. T 10. T
Part 3: 11. T 12. F 13. T
Part 4: 14. F 15. T 16. F 17. T
Part 5: 18. T 19. T 20. F 21. T

7. LOOKING AT LANGUAGE
1. b 2. a 3. a 4. a 5. b 6. a 7. a 8. b

8. FOLLOW-UP ACTIVITIES
A. Taking Notes to Prepare

	Years Ago	Today
Smoker's attitudes toward their smoking:	• didn't give a lot of thought to it	• keenly aware of others' preceptions • realize it's much less popular
Smoking at people's homes:	• fifteen years ago people offered an ashtray at their house	• smokers don't even ask to smoke • people wish smokers wouldn't smoke in their homes
Smoking at parties:	• cocktail and cigarette and blabbing were normal	• smokers smoke furtively around window or outside
Smokers' habits:	• smoking in someone's office was OK	• would never think of having a cigarette in someone's office • body language in groups: —blow smoke up —hold cigarette out

UNIT 2

A Wine That's Raised Some Stink

3. VOCABULARY
1. top 2. bad breath 3. reproduced 4. imitation 5. transportation 6. smell 7. sweet 8. fact 9. kitchen 10. exciting 11. employer

4. TASK LISTENING
Garlic.

5. LISTENING FOR MAIN IDEAS
Suggested answers:
Part 1: The winery made garlic wine because garlic grows in its region.

Part 2: Garlic wine is made from a secret formula.
Part 3: People don't think it tastes like wine.

6. LISTENING FOR DETAILS
Part 1: 1. b   2. c   3. c   4. a
Part 2: 5. b   6. c   7. a   8. b
Part 3: 9. a   10. c   11. a

7. LOOKING AT LANGUAGE
1. wine   2. time   3. about   4. can   5. let / about
6. some   7. town   8. is   9. wine   11. And / fine
13. Share   14. And / time

8. FOLLOW-UP ACTIVITIES
A. Taking Notes to Prepare
THE DESIGN
Local resources used:
* California garlic
Description of the product:
* you can smell the garlic
* familiar taste
* tastes like something you'd put on your salad
* bit of a tang to it
* tastes like Pine Sol™
* tastes like salad dressing
* it's dry
The label:
* promises "an experience that never leaves you breathless"
Research and development:
* family staff wanted to contribute to garlic capital
* experimented for one year
* derived a secret formula
  * garlic essence, powder, or fresh garlic
MARKETING
Taste trends and fashion:
* wine is fun
* not necessarily a stuffy product
Pricing:
* $5.00 a bottle
Promotion of product:
* wrote "The Garlic Song"

UNIT 3
Drive-In Shopping

3. VOCABULARY
1. h   2. k   3. j   4. b   5. i   6. a   7. g   8. d   9. f
10. l   11. e   12. c

4. TASK LISTENING
To save time.

5. LISTENING FOR MAIN IDEAS
Suggested answers:
Part 1: A new drive-in supermarket is saving time for shoppers in California.
Part 2: The successful ideas of drive-through convenience and catalog shopping were applied to grocery shopping.
Part 3: There are disadvantages to this time-saving system of grocery shopping.
Part 4: Drive-in supermarkets could be the way of shopping throughout the United States in the future.

6. LISTENING FOR DETAILS
Part 1: 1. F   2. T   3. T   4. F   5. T
Part 2: 6. T   7. F   8. F   9. T   10. F   11. F   12. F
Part 3: 13. F   14. F   15. T   16. F   17. F   18. T
Part 4: 19. F   20. F   21. F   22. T

7. LOOKING AT LANGUAGE

Taste	**Smell**	**Touch**	**Sight**	**Hearing**
sip	sniff	squeeze	spot	overhear
lick	inhale	rub	catch	eavesdrop
savor	savor	grasp	sight of	perceive
	take a whiff	fondle	notice	
		handle	witness	
		pinch	glimpse	
		stroke	stare	
			perceive	

8. FOLLOW-UP ACTIVITIES
A. Taking Notes to Prepare
The service:
* drive-in supermarket
The location:
* near the intersection of two major L.A. freeways
The number of cars that can be accommodated:
* 300 cars per hour
The ordering procedure:
* make up grocery list from catalog
* phone in item numbers
* drive up three hours later
The use of computers:
* computer prints out grocery list
* workers follow numbers through a warehouse
* customers punch code into terminal and write checks

The disadvantages to consider:
- can't sniff the fish or squeeze the melon
- only fancy-grade produce
- perishables kept in freezer or refrigerators until pickup
- $1.50 service charge

The prices:
- prices are comparable to other grocery stores'

UNIT 4

Is It a Sculpture, Or Is It Food?

3. VOCABULARY
11, 7, 8, 5, 6, 4, 2, 1, 10, 9, 3

4. TASK LISTENING
She's more against it.

5. LISTENING FOR MAIN IDEAS
Suggested answers:
Part 1: Chefs from around the country have boycotted genetically engineered food.
Part 2: Joyce Goldstein is concerned about the consequences of genetically altered foods such as the tomato.
Part 3: Without proper labeling and sufficient testing, we currently have a lack of information about genetically engineered foods.
Part 4: Goldstein feels we have the right to know whether foods on the market have been genetically engineered.

6. LISTENING FOR DETAILS
Part 1: 1. F   2. T   3. T   4. T   5. F   6. T
Part 2: 7. F   8. F   9. T
Part 3: 10. F   11. F   12. T   13. T   14. F   15. T   16. F
Part 4: 17. T   18. T   19. F   20. T   21. F   22. F

7. LOOKING AT LANGUAGE
In the near future, you might be able to buy a tomato in the supermarket that has been genetically designed and engineered, a tomato that would stay ripe much longer, strawberries that are not so fragile in freezing temperatures, vegetable oil that's lower in fat. Already on the market: a gene-spliced product that's used in cheese making. There are impressive claims being made for genetic manipulation of food, including production increases that could help alleviate world hunger. But there's also concern, and indeed some fear, about the use of gene-splicing techniques. . . .

8. FOLLOW-UP ACTIVITIES
A. Taking Notes to Prepare
Benefits of genetic engineering:
- longer-life tomato
- less fragile strawberries
- roses—beautiful
- improved and safe product
- boon for corporate profit
- no pesticides

Disadvantages of genetic engineering:
- gene-splicing techniques not clear
- no special labeling for such food
- no testing—nonknowledge
- allergies
- possible lack of taste
- health issue unclear
- profit over consumer safety and needs

UNIT 5

Gang Violence

3. VOCABULARY
1. d   2. h   3. e   4. c   5. f   6. i   7. j   8. a
9. b   10. g

4. TASK LISTENING
Yes.

5. LISTENING FOR MAIN IDEAS
Suggested answers:
Part 1: There are a large number of gangs in Chicago.
Part 2: They always fight in groups.
Part 3: Kids join gangs to find some identity.
Part 4: Gangs identify themselves with hand-signals.
Part 5: Bill Recktenwald suggests that the community get together to control gangs.

6. LISTENING FOR DETAILS
Part 1: 1. T   2. T   3. F   4. F   5. T
Part 2: 6. T   7. F   8. F   9. T   10. T
Part 3: 11. F   12. T   13. F   14. T   15. F
Part 4: 16. F   17. F   18. T
Part 5: 19. T   20. F   21. T   22. T

8. FOLLOW-UP ACTIVITIES
A. Taking Notes to Prepare
Description of gangs:
- under age 20
- individuals afraid to stand alone
- cowards
- fight in groups of six or seven

- ambush or shoot at people
- chase each other and fire
- innocent children get killed

Reason for gangs:
- looking for identity
- makes them feel big and tough
- want to be like the pimp
  - car
  - fur coat
- want to make lots of money

Gang rituals:
- signaling your group affiliation
  - hand signals
    - upwards = member of gang
    - downwards = death to the gang

What neighborhood watch clubs can do:
- start a block club
- graffiti watch
- telephone chains to police and neighbors
- volunteer to be a witness
- appear in court to represent neighborhood

UNIT 6

Create Controversy to Generate Publicity

3. VOCABULARY
1. k 2. b 3. j 4. l 5. f 6. h 7. g 8. i 9. a
10. d 11. c 12. e

4. TASK LISTENING
Forty-nine dollars.

5. LISTENING FOR MAIN IDEAS
Suggested answers:
Part 1: Benetton has produced a set of controversial ads.
Part 2: The ads create controversy and generate publicity for the company.
Part 3: Some say the ad of the newborn is disgusting, while others say it is natural.
Part 4: According to Garfield, the ads benefit publicity while they distract consumers from Benetton's high prices.

6. LISTENING FOR DETAILS
Part 1: 1. a 2. c 3. a
Part 2: 4. b 5. c
Part 3: 6. b 7. c
Part 4: 8. b 9. a 10. c 11. b 12. c

---

8. FOLLOW-UP ACTIVITIES
A. Taking Notes to Prepare
Benetton's purpose behind the ads:
- create controversy and generate publicity
- enhance consumer exposure to their natural habitat
- to tick people off
- inflame consumer outrage
- publicity benefit
- distraction marketing

Public reaction to the ads:
- look at them seriously
- anger or disgust
- arresting; makes you stop cold
- magnificent and natural?
- magazines are awfully touchy?

Other magazines' publishing decisions for Benetton ads:
- *Essence* and *Child*: rejected the ad with the children
- *Self*: – published baby
          – refused nun
- *Cosmo*: didn't publish newborn baby

UNIT 7

Women Caught in the Middle of Two Generations

3. VOCABULARY
4, 2, 7, 9, 6, 10, 3, 5, 8, 1

4. TASK LISTENING
Middle-aged women.

5. LISTENING FOR MAIN IDEAS
Suggested answers:
Part 1: In America, children are becoming the caretakers of their parents.
Part 2: As aging parents move into their children's homes, they become their constant companions.
Part 3: It is difficult for women to express the anger they feel in their role as caretakers.
Part 4: They resent being put in the mother role again.
Part 5: It's not an easy choice to put a parent in a nursing home.

6. LISTENING FOR DETAILS
Part 1: 1. F 2. F 3. F
Part 2: 4. F 5. F 6. T 7. F 8. F 9. F
10. T

Part 3: 11. F 12. F 13. T 14. F 15. T
Part 4: 16. F 17. T 18. F 19. F
Part 5: 20. T 21. T 22. T 23. F 24. F

7. LOOKING AT LANGUAGE
The following verbs can be replaced by the *would* verb form:
3, 7, 8, 9, 11, 12, 15

8. FOLLOW-UP ACTIVITIES
A. Taking Notes to Prepare

	Decisions	*Feelings*
Susan:	• brought her blind mother-in-law home • took her everywhere; constant companion • placed her mother-in-law in a nursing home	• felt stress on her marriage • angry about losing control • felt trapped • whole life changed • doesn't want to live with her children
Margaret:	• would fly off to take care of mother • placed her mother in a nursing home	• felt role-reversal with dependent mother • felt mother was like a retarded child • doesn't want to live with her children
Vivian:	• took on full-time job of caretaking for her mother • placed her mother in a nursing home	• felt she could only stay away for short periods • sense of duty • shame at resenting duty • tired of being a mother • doesn't want to live with children

UNIT 8
The Mail-Order Bride

3. VOCABULARY
1. c 2. d 3. g 4. b 5. i 6. h 7. e 8. a
9. f

4. TASK LISTENING
They come from the Philippines and Malaysia.

5. LISTENING FOR MAIN IDEAS
Suggested answers:
Part 1: Asian women are coming to the United States to marry American men.
Part 2: American men choose these women because they think Asian women are more feminine than American women.

Part 3: The men and women are matched by a profile form.
Part 4: Louis Florence thinks his service helps people get to know each other better.

6. LISTENING FOR DETAILS
Part 1: 1. b 2. c 3. b
Part 2: 4. b 5. c 6. c
Part 3: 7. b 8. a
Part 4: 9. b 10. c

7. LOOKING AT LANGUAGE
1. d 2. b 3. f 4. a 5. c 6. g 7. e

8. FOLLOW-UP ACTIVITIES
A. Taking Notes to Prepare
The interviewer's point of view (questions/concerns about the service):

- Do Asian women have a corner on knowing how to please?
- This seems to come out all in one direction.
- Are there any protections for the women here?
- How did personality profile get made up?
- Why are certain questions asked?
    - –polishing toenails
    - –size of breasts
- Critics say Florences are peddling flesh.

The Florences' point of view (benefits offered by the service):

- The men feel like they're on their honeymoon after four or five years.
- Asian women will love, honor, obey, and treat their husbands very nicely all the time.
- Personality profile asks questions that men cannot afford to ask the ladies.
    - –make up
    - –sexuality
- It offers alternative to common methods of meeting somebody of opposite sex.
    - –singles bar = flesh market
    - –church. . .
    - –men and women can write letters with service
        - without touching
        - pour heart out
- Their marriages are working out.

UNIT 9

Facing the Wrong End of a Pistol

3. VOCABULARY
Exercise 1
1. i 2. g 3. a 4. h 5. b 6. d 7. c 8. f
9. e
Exercise 2

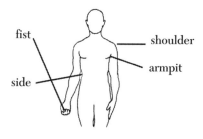

4. TASK LISTENING
He is in favor of gun control.

5. LISTENING FOR MAIN IDEAS
Suggested answers:
Part 1: Some people are trying to stop the sale of Saturday Night Specials.
Part 2: Olen Kelley was held up and shot.
Part 3: He's suing a manufacturer of Saturday Night Specials.

6. LISTENING FOR DETAILS
Part 1: 1. b 2. b 3. c 4. c
Part 2: 5. a 6. b
Part 3: 7. c 8. b 9. c 10. c 11. c

7. LOOKING AT LANGUAGE
Exercise 1
1. missed 2. time 3. head 4. hammer
5. down 6. open 7. floor 8. lay 9. over
10. sure

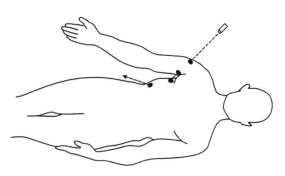

Exercise 2

8. FOLLOW-UP ACTIVITIES
A. Taking Notes to Prepare
Kelley's background:
- grocery store manager in Silver Spring, Maryland
- held up five times
- robbers had guns each time

The holdup:
- two men after money in store's safe
- Kelley missed the combination the first time
- robbers put gun to his head
- Kelley got safe open
- robbers told him to get down on the floor
- Kelley lay down
- they hit him over the head
- shot him
    - –in shoulder
    - –bullet came out armpit
    - –traveled down side
    - –came out lower side

The suit:
- suing distributor
  - –in Florida
  - –maker (Relm) is in Germany
- not after NRA or sporting-type guns; after junk guns
- willing to go to Supreme Court if necessary
- $500 million damages from RG industries

UNIT 10
What Constitutes a Family?

3. VOCABULARY
1. volunteer-working   2. member   3. biological parents   4. nuclear family   5. light   6. rise
7. middle-aged   8. fought against   9. ignore
10. invite   11. cancel   12. guardian

4. TASK LISTENING
possible examples:
gay couples, foster parents, stepfamilies, labor unions, historical societies, unrelated seniors

5. LISTENING FOR MAIN IDEAS
Suggested answers:
Part 1: California now publicly registers nontraditional groups as families.
Part 2: Shannon Gibson has both a biological father and a stepfather in her family.
Part 3: The courts will be grappling with the issue of what constitutes a family.
Part 4: It could help legitimize his status as a single father with dependents.

6. LISTENING FOR DETAILS
Part 1: 1. a   2. a
Part 2: 3. c   4. c   5. c   6. b
Part 3: 7. b   8. a   9. b   10. c
Part 4: 11. b   12. c   13. b   14. a

8. FOLLOW-UP ACTIVITIES
A. Taking Notes to Prepare
Examples of nontraditional families:
- gay couples
- foster parents
- stepfamilies
- labor unions
- historical societies
- unrelated seniors

Reasons nontraditional families want to register as a family:
- visitation rights
- housing rights
- health benefits
- tax returns

UNIT 11
Finding Discrimination Where One Would Hope to Find Relief

3. VOCABULARY
15, 5, 7, 1, 8, 13, 3, 6, 10, 9, 11, 2, 14, 4, 12

4. TASK LISTENING
He's more sympathetic.

5. LISTENING FOR MAIN IDEAS
Suggested answers:
Part 1: We can find discrimination against AIDS victims in the nation's courtrooms and insurance companies.
Part 2: The courts convict criminals with AIDS with unduly harsh sentences, probably out of irrational fear.
Part 3: Insurance companies and employers won't insure AIDS victims or will not offer enough coverage.
Part 4: Much of this discrimination comes from economics.
Part 5: Gosten sees AIDS discrimination as similar to racial discrimination.

6. LISTENING FOR DETAILS
Part 1: 1. b   2. a
Part 2: 3. c   4. b   5. a   6. c
Part 3: 7. a   8. c
Part 4: 9. c   10. b
Part 5: 11. a   12. b

7. LOOKING AT LANGUAGE
1. by   2. for   3. on   4. on   5. for   6. for   7. from   8. from   9. against   10. against   11. to   12. from   13. to   14. about

8. FOLLOW-UP ACTIVITIES
A. Taking Notes to Prepare
The courts:
- reinforce myths about how AIDS is transmitted
- judges rule spitting and biting as serious crimes when accused has AIDS
- no case where AIDS was actually transmitted
- irrational fear of transmission
- focus is on "intent"
- suicide case: victim splattered blood as cry for help; given four life sentences; will die in prison

Insurance companies:
- people can't afford the treatments
- won't insure AIDS patients
- say health benefits plan will be overburdened

Employers:
- changed health care benefits when discovered employee had AIDS (only $5,000 coverage)
- say they can't hire an AIDS victim because clients won't come
- say they lack the clinical expertise to handle AIDS victims

Society:
- discrimination springs from a deep place
- people's own fear of getting the disease and dying
- stems from economics
- similar to racial discrimination (seen as repugnant)

UNIT 12

Green Consumerism

3. VOCABULARY

10, 11, 2, 7, 1, 9, 4, 5, 6, 3, 8

4. TASK LISTENING

Product	False Advertising Promise
gasoline	eat good cereal
cars	save the environment
candy	encourage new values

gasoline — eat good cereal
cars ✕ save the environment
candy — encourage new values

5. LISTENING FOR MAIN IDEAS

Suggested answers:

Part 1: Consumers may feel a false sense of complacency by only shopping differently.

Part 2: One thing we can do to help the environment is turn our shopping cart into a vehicle for social change when we go shopping.

Part 3: Overconsumption by advanced industrial countries is a longer-term issue that we must focus on to save the earth.

Part 4: We have to be careful of the green marketing that is going on and the hucksters who profit from it.

Part 5: We should think about revitalizing our transportation systems rather than which new car to buy.

6. LISTENING FOR DETAILS

Part 1: 1. c 2. a 3. c
Part 2: 4. a 5. c
Part 3: 6. b 7. b 8. b 9. c
Part 4: 10. b 11. a 12. a 13. c
Part 5: 14. c 15. c 16. a 17. a

7. LOOKING AT LANGUAGE

Answers will vary.

8. FOLLOW-UP ACTIVITIES

A. Taking Notes to Prepare

Consumption:
- we should consume less   +
- turn shopping cart into a vehicle for social change   +
- shift our emphasis from gross consumption to more subtle lifestyle   +

Planting the earth:
- grow for ourselves what we need   +
- throw waste in compost heap   +
- plant a tree seedling   –

Education and public policy:
- green consuming as an initial educational step   +
- consumers need to be well informed   +
- federal-level guidelines for labels   +

Recycling:
- Yuppies can do their part recycling bottles and newspapers   –

Transportation:
- buy a Toyota as an example of new values (e.g., fuel-efficient)   –
- reform transportation systems   +
- revitalize public transportation, rail transportation   +

PHOTO CREDITS

We wish to thank the following for providing us with photographs: